Dieter Graf

Naxos
& Small Cyclades

Náxos

Donoússa
Iráklia
Koufonísi
Schinoússa

The 36 most beautiful walks
on 5 Greek Islands

Graf Editions

Using this illustrated walking guide

AWT stands for Actual Walking Time – excluding any breaks! The AWT serves as a personal control as to whether certain route sections, emphasised in **bold print**, have been reached roughly within the given time.
The approximate **overall length** of a walk is *about twice as long as the AWT* and is specified in hours in the introduction to each tour. These figures do not include time taken for bus trips or extra-long breaks. Information concerning the **length of the walks,** the **difference in altitude (elevation gain)** and the **three levels of difficulty** can also be found.
Route photos are intended for orientation, for consulting locals and as a stimulus. The corresponding text is marked by 1 to 4.
The **route sketches** have been drawn to the best of our knowledge but lay no claim to completeness.
GPS points are shown as P in texts and on maps. Map datum WGS 84.
The **overview diagrams** at the end of the book make it easier to decide on the appropriate tour.

We would be grateful for useful information concerning **changes** in paths and similar data. As a token of our appreciation we will send you a free copy of our next edition.
The website www.graf-editions.de informs you of changes that occur along walking routes.

The author Dieter Graf is an architect who has travelled all over the world. He has walked the Aegean Islands since the years when tourism was just beginning there and is considered a connoisseur of the islands.

All the hiking trails have been described to the best of the author's knowledge. Walking the routes described in this book is at the hiker's own risk. It is therefore not possible to assume liability for accidents or damage of any kind.

Edition Dieter Graf, Elisabethstr. 29, 80796 Muenchen, Germany
www.graf-editions.de

Typesetting: Michael Henn, Hersbruck · Maps: Kurt Zucher, Eckersdorf

Translation: Myles Oliver, Muenchen

Original Title: »Wandern auf Griechischen Inseln: Naxos & Kleine Kykladen« (ISBN 978-3-9819250-0-5)

Cover Photo: Ágios Georgios & Panagía ⑥

ISBN 978-3-9819250-1-2

Contents

Náxos

Already when you sail into the harbour, you can sense the tremendous cultural diversity of the largest of the Cyclades islands. On the left, you peer up at the enormous portal of a classical temple; on the right, you glide past a small Byzantine chapel and, towering above the huddled Cycladic city, a Venetian kástro from the Middle Ages. The city, dating back 6000 years, is one of the oldest inhabited places in the world.

Νάξος

When you penetrate further in to the island, you are surprised by the diversity of the fertile landscapes. An enormous rugged mountain massif – consisting of granite, gneiss and marble with three peaks rising to an altitude of almost 1000 metres – forms the background for the green heart of the island, the Tragéa plain, covered with olive groves and ancient oaks. Stretching further westwards is extensive farming land, until it meets a never-ending landscape of dunes along the seaside. Connoisseurs of small bathing bays are more likely to find wonderful spots along the rocky east coast. To this day ancient mule tracks criss-cross this landscape, making Náxos a favourite for hikers.

However, it is not just nature which surprises with its enormous abundance. People have also left outstanding buildings during their long habitation of the island. Besides the lively Mediterranean, almost Oriental harbour city, we find compact mountain villages which allow us, even today, to trace the tracks of old Greece. Whitewashed cubic houses and narrow, marbled alleys set the tone here. Art-lovers find not only the remains of Ionic temples, but also monumental statues worked on by artists and left behind in ancient quarries. The Byzantine chapels from a later period house Early Medieval frescoes. In addition, there are also a great number of castle-like residences from the Venetian nobility of the Middle Ages. The Venetians, rulers of the island for 300 years, also built Catholic monasteries. All these sights are included on the walks described here!

For many visitors Náxos is the most beautiful island of the Cyclades, not least because it has been spared mass tourism. One finds hotels of every standard, but no over-developed resorts. The pleasantly relaxed hospitality extended here will remain in the memory for a long while.

April 2018 Dieter Graf

Have a good trip *Kaló taxídi*!

Walking on Náxos

Thanks to its varied landscape and lush vegetation, which distinguishes it from most of the other, more barren Cyclades, Náxos is one of the finest hiking islands in Greece. Moreover, the hiker still finds many intact old **mule tracks.** For centuries these narrow ***monopátia*** (sing. *monopáti*) used to help the farmers work the fields and, up until 30 years ago, formed a dense network of tracks (see p. 29 ③).
By contrast, the up to four metre wide paved tracks, the ***kalderímia,*** connected larger villages for the transport of goods and served as paths for pilgrims to the monasteries. They were paved with marble and bordered with walls. Some of them are said to be up to 1000 years old (see p. 50 ②).
Motorisation has not failed to leave its mark on the islands either. Instead of mules the farmers now use pickups, which require wider roadways. The old network of tracks was torn apart by broadening the mule tracks to make them accessible to cars wherever it seemed to be necessary and by pushing aside the characteristic dry walls along the waysides, all co-financed by money from the European Union Regional Funds. The remaining paths are now superfluous and in ruins and are gradually being forgotten by the islanders. Lately, however, the EU Leader Fund provides money to restore some of the remaining mule tracks, mainly for the sake of tourism. Instead of maintaining and extending the scope of the network, however, this often only amounts to the over-perfect restoration of individual paths. This book aims to help ensure that the old mule tracks which still exist are used again and hence preserved before they are irreparably destroyed. They may, above all in spring, be rather overgrown!
All the routes described have been walked along again shortly before publication and can be followed without difficulty by people in normal physical condition. Some of the walks are suitable for children. Special surefootedness is not necessary. The ✓-markings in the text concern only those who are very afraid of heights. For longer walking tours **short cuts** are indicated. Due to the good views, the tours normally lead from the mountains to the sea – so take along your swimming gear. You should be absolutely sure to pick a nice day for tours in the mountains since there is always the danger of sudden fog formation. Moreover it can rain there even in summer. On the other hand there is a risk of bush fires in the summer.
If you want to walk alone, you should by all means leave information in your hotel and save the number of the hotel on your

mobile phone. In order to get your blood circulation going, you should begin leisurely and, during the tour, eat and especially drink often, even if you don't feel the need to do so. The route maps show springs and wells to be found by the wayside. Be sure to protect yourself sufficiently against sun and wind too.

The island administration now organizes the clearing of old paths and fixing of wooden signs or numbered, miniature red-and-white metal signs as **route markings.** Coloured dots and cairns are also in evidence, but do not necessarily match the descriptions in this book.

Good **Náxos maps** are offered by the Greek publishers Anavási, Skaï-Terrain and Orama at a scale of 1:40,000. On the rear side of the Anavási map, moreover, the Small Cyclades are depicted at a scale of 1:25,000.

As new roadways continue to be built, it may be that the route descriptions are partly out of date, thus calling for certain **orientation skills.** If you have orientation problems, you should always ask the locals about the "monopáti", otherwise you will be directed to roads for vehicular traffic.

Mule dung on the narrow paths is more certain to lead you further than goat droppings since the goat paths usually end somewhere in the scrub, while mules always return to their stalls.

If you lose your way, you may have to shin up a field wall or climb over steel mesh used as grazing fences with the help of a pile of stones. Pasture fences are knotted shut on the side where there are two perpendicular rods. You owe it to the farmers whose land you walk across to shut the openings again afterwards, of course. Access to the sea is allowed in Greece as a matter of principle.

Almost all the starting and finishing points are served by **public buses,** even in the low season until mid-May. In case a service does not operate on Saturdays or Sundays, take a taxi. You should settle the price before you begin the trip. In addition, car drivers also enjoy taking along a wanderer who waves him down.

Users of **hire cars** find the parking place in the maps of this book under the symbol 🚗. Where the description does not feature a circular hike, a scheduled bus will bring you back to your car. Circular hikes can easily be found in the **overview diagrams** at the back of the book. These also contain information about the physical and time requirements for the various walks.

Walks which are particularly recommended:
3 5 12 13 14 18 19 22 25

Appropriate **hiking gear** includes a daypack, shoes with good soles (no sandals), comfortable socks, long trousers or zipper trousers*, possibly telescope sticks, mobile phone, binoculars, a small flashlight, picnic equipment with salt-shaker, energy bar, magnesium, plaster, string. In the spring and autumn, rainwear is a necessity. A GPS device would also be good, but is not necessary if you have a fairly good sense of orientation.
*The legs of zipper trousers which also have vertical zippers can be zipped together to form a pad to sit on at the beach. And if you connect both zippers, you have a chic skirt for visiting monasteries.

■ **Emergency telephone numbers:** Taxi 0030-22850-22444/-24331, fire service -32199, international 112

Climate and Walking Seasons

The climate on Náxos corresponds to that on the other Cyclades with a hot and dry summer and a mild rainy winter. The maximum **air temperature** is 32° C in August (at night 22° C). In the walking months May/June and September temperatures range between 19° and 24°. In winter the temperature sinks to 15° C (7° C) in February. On mountains above 800 m snow can fall and lie for a short while, most recently in the winter of 2016/17.
The **water temperatures** vary between 16° C in February and almost 25° C in August. You can go swimming from the end of May at 19° C through to October (22° C).
The **rainy days** are spread irregularly throughout the year. Most of the rain falls in December and January, when it rains on about 14 days. You must still calculate with 3 days of rain in May, while there is absolute dryness from June to August. Statistically September has 2 and October 6 days of rain, but it is not very plentiful.
The number of **hours of sunshine** per day corresponds to this pattern. In December and January the very strong winter sun only shines for about 4½ hours. Even in May the wanderer must reconcile himself to 10 hours of sunshine per day and the swimmer to 12 in August. October is once again pleasant for autumn walkers, with 7¾ hours of sunshine per day.
The Cyclades mainly have strong **north winds**, although Náxos is somewhat protected from these by having Mýkonos off the north coast. One reason for this is the difference in air pressure between the Azore highs and the hot low pressure areas above the Persian Gulf. In the transition season, especially in April and May and then October and November, the *Boréas* dominates, a cool, wet north wind. In the summer (May to September) the famous etesien winds, called the *meltémia,* blow up to force five or

six and normally abate towards evening. All the same, the sea remains relatively calm and the sky clear but misty. The sirocco occurs less frequently, but especially in spring. It comes from the hot Sahara desert, picking up moisture over the Mediterranean to bring the Aegean warm humidity.

On the Greek islands there are several different **seasons for walking** tours. Anyone wishing to feast his eyes should plan his tour around Easter. It might be somewhat cool and even muddy, but the countryside is grass-green, poppy-red and broom-yellow; the houses and alleyways are freshly whitewashed. The preparations for the Greek Easter celebration alone make the trip worthwhile. However, you can't go swimming yet, and some hotels and tavernas are still closed. In April it can rain briefly. The Greeks divide the year into three parts, and this one is called "the time of blossoming and maturing".

In May and June the blossom time is already partially over, but, since it is very warm and the number of tourists is still limited, this is probably the most attractive time for walking. Beginning at the end of May the water has a pleasant temperature.

The main tourist season in July and August is not highly recommended for walking tours due to the heat. It is the "dry period" in Greece. The dry north winds, which blow continuously, still make the temperatures bearable, but at noon it is wise to seek a shady spot under a tree. Harvest time begins in July. On 15th August, the Assumption of the Virgin, called "Passing Away Peacefully" in the Eastern Church, there are great celebrations everywhere with roast lamb, music and dance.

From the beginning of September on, the heat is over and the sea still has a pleasant temperature for swimming, up until the end of October. Now it is again possible to take longer walking tours, but only until about 6 pm due to the shorter period of daylight. The land has become yellow and brown, the fields bear their fruit, and everywhere you meet friendly farmers harvesting their last crops. From the beginning of October on, it can start to rain again. The restaurants and hotels gradually shut down and some owners travel to their winter residences in Athens. Others put on camouflage suits, reach for their guns and search through the undergrowth. A million Greeks are passionate hunters. In November there is usually a change in climate, with heavy rainfall. Then it becomes unpleasant. The period from November to February is called the "rain season". Although there are some warm, sunny days around Christmas, it is more pleasant at home.

Geology

The Aegean Sea was not flooded by the sea until after the last ice age. Up until then the present island arc between Crete and Rhodes formed the southern edge of the mainland.
The more northern Cycladic islands stand on a submarine mountain which was raised out of the sea 50 million years ago by the pressure of the African continental plate on the European continental plate. After repeated earth-shifts the islands assumed their current form. That is why one encounters slate, a sedimentary rock which was lifted out of the sea and sits on top of a bed of marble and granite. Náxos is especially rich in marble. Embedded inside this is auburn emery, an extremely hard and heavy conglomerate consisting of magnetic iron ore, mica and corundum. The emery in the north of Náxos is the best natural emery in the world (see p. 104).
On the southern edge of the Aegean an active seismic arc extends from the Peleponnesus via the islands Póros, Mílos, Santoríni, Anáfi, Níssiros and Kos as far as the Taurus mountain range in Turkey. The pressure created by the land masses discharges itself here now and again as earthquakes. Half the earthquakes in Europe occur in Greece. Náxos, however, is seismically quieter.

Fauna

In contrast to the flora the variety of the animal kingdom is limited. As a result of the mostly low vegetation large game is not encountered. Hares and martens are seldom. The animals one most often comes across are goats and sheep, though not in such large numbers as in former years. Sometimes even pasture land is burned off, in order to create fresh nutriments for goats. The few cows have an almost exotic charm. Together with the goats they supply the milk for the island's extremely sophisticated cheeses. A further famous natural product on Náxos is supplied by the bees – thyme honey. Of the smaller animals one hears and sees the small common lizard, which can be up to 10 cm long. The dragon-like agama (hardun) [1] its bigger relative, is up to 30 cm long. Even land turtles have now become rare.
The careful wanderer will rarely see snakes. There is only one poisonous type: the horn or sand viper [2]. It can be up to 50 cm long and as thick as two thumbs. A healthy adult hardly need fear a deadly bite.
The non-poisonous sand-boa is about the same size. The non-poisonous four-striped-adder reaches an adult length of more

than a metre and a width almost as thick as an arm. Its size is frightening, but it is harmless, as is the ring-snake. As long as one does not move completely silently, the snakes disappear again. Long trousers give additional protection. On no account should one lift up large stones, as snakes may be sleeping underneath them.

The up to 5 cm long scorpions also hide there. The bite of a scorpion is rather painful but not deadly. They also love to hide in shoes. You can rouse crabs, frogs and eels along the watercourses. In rocky bays you should look out for sea urchins 3.

Soaring above in search of prey are birds such as buzzards, falcons and griffon vultures; unfortunately migratory birds often fall victim to the Greek passion for hunting.

Flora

Ever since antiquity forests on the Aegean islands have been cut down for building ships or have fallen victim to forest fires in summer, causing some parts of the countryside to seem like karstland. This effect is intensified by the limestone soil which cannot store water. Nevertheless, along with Spain, Greece has

the greatest variety of plants in Europe. While there may be no forest hikes, it is still possible to find shady trails in the Pláka between the tall windbreaks made of reeds (p. 40).

The **stock of trees** consists mainly solitary specimens. Besides Aleppo pines [1] tall evergreen oaks and kermes oaks [2] grow in protected regions which are rich in water. Unassuming, salt-tolerant tamarisks [3] are found along beaches. Plane-trees [4] shade the village squares and slender cypresses the cemeteries. Acacias, poplars, alders, maples and eucalyptus trees [5] can also be found, as well as mulberry trees [6] and carobs [7]. Among the fruit trees there are pomegranates, fig trees [8] and citrus fruits. Yet dominating the landscape most of all is the olive tree, which looks strangely deformed as it gets older.

In the open countryside dry shrubs reaching a height of up to half a metre predominate, thorny undergrowth (garrigue) called **phrýgana** in Greek. Typical representatives of this "low macchia" are broom, thorny knap-weed, heather, spiny spurge plants (euphorbia) [9] [10] plants often shaped like hedgehogs. Jerusalem sage, squill and asphodel [12] blossom there.

Thicker bush or tree groups up to two metres high with evergreens and bushes with hard leaves are not found as frequently.

10

11

12

This "high macchia" is called xerovoúmi in Greek. Kermes oaks with serrated leaves [2], juniper and mastic bushes [11] are particularly predominant. Mastic bushes are used for manufacturing rubber and raki spirits.
The keeping of goats has caused the beginnings of higher vegetation to be kept low. Sometimes grazing land is burned to give the goats the freshly growing sprouts as food. Inedible plants such as Jerusalem sage, squill or asphodel [12] grow here quickly. The agave [13], attributed to the cactus family, often lines the lanes and paths. This thorny leaf plant has only grown in the Mediterranean area since the 16th century. The fruit of the fig-cactus [14] makes a sweet supplement to any hiker's picnic.
Flowers can mainly be appreciated in spring. Already in January the anemone and crocus blossom. Then, from February through to May/June, all the splendour of white and red blossoming rockroses [15], iris, yellow daffodils, hyacinths, lupines, chrysanthemums and broom add magic to the landscape with their cheery colours, and the poppy adds its bright red.
Small orchids are an adornment of spring for a short time. The bee orchid (ophrys) [16], lax-flowered orchid (orchis), tongue orchid (serapias) and dragon arum, also called "Dead Horse" on ac-

13

14

15

count of the smell [17], can be seen frequently.
In May and June the main blossoming season comes to an end, but summer doesn't mean brown wilderness by any means. Bougainvillea radiates its bright colours on the house walls (p. 137), and oleander blossoms in moist spots. The thorny acanthus [18] and the gold thistle [19] bloom along the wayside.
In the late summer and autumn the flora begins to come alive again and blossom after the first brief rain showers. Meadow-saffron, heather and squill reveal themselves along with the dandelions, thistles and cyclamen.
Many of the plants contain ethereal oils. In the heat of the day you can especially appreciate the pleasantly spicy aroma of thyme, rosemary, lavender, oregano, camomile and fennel. Sage [20], capers [21] and other kitchen herbs often border the paths.
Farming has been carried on since the third pre-Christian millennium. Good opportunities for irrigation and flat areas are more conducive to farming than on the other Cyclades. Cultivated on the coastal plains are mainly cereals, vegetables and the renowned potatoes. In higher areas are as many as 270,000 olive trees, half of them on the Tragéa plain. Wine is cultivated mostly in the north.

A brief history

Prehistoric time The Cyclades have been settled since the Mesolithic period (7500 BC). The Influence of Mesopotamia and early Middle Eastern civilizations came to Europe via the Aegean islands. During the transition to the Bronze Age Europe there experiences its first artistic climax, the Cycladic culture (3200-1100 BC). The seemingly modern, up to 1.50m tall, originally painted flat female figures made of marble are famous. The most important finds have been made on Náxos, on Sýros and the now uninhabited Kéros (Small Cyclades).
Four thousand years ago the Phoenicians arrive from the coast of what is now Lebanon. They impart the skills of the Assyrians and Babylonians to the Greeks, as well as introducing writing and money. Then the islands come under the influence of Minoan Crete and, after its decline around 1450 BC, of Mycenae. On the mainland the Dorians, probably migrating from Dalmatia, later trigger a migration of peoples. After 1200 BC the islands of the Aegean and Asia Minor are colonized from there in several waves. Náxos and the northern Cyclades are dominated by the Ionians.

Archaic Period (800–500 BC The Ionians are the first to release the Greek spirit in the sense of artistic, intellectual and economic freedom. In the sixth century BC the leadership of Greek culture is found on the islands. The mainland does not adopt these ideas until later. In terms of architecture it seems that stone temples were built on the islands much earlier – especially on Náxos. Náxos also founds the first Greek colony on Sicily. Náxos attains its greatest influence under the ruler Lygdamis, a "tyrant" in the original, not negative sense, around 550 BC, when it already has 100,000 inhabitants, today it has 20,000.
Starting in 540 BC, the Persian Empire extends its influence to the coast of Asia Minor. Athens makes Délos the intellectual and cultural centre of the Attic-Delian maritime alliance. This protective league against Persia unites the Greeks in the Aegean and Asia Minor with Athens. War is unavoidable and begins in 490 BC. Already in the same year Náxos is ravaged by the Persians and is obliged to give military assistance.

The Classical Period (490–336 BC) Náxos therefore fights on the opposite side at the beginning of the Persian Wars, but is on Athens' side for the final triumph over the Persians in 449 BC. Immense riches are amassed on Délos during the "Golden Age" which follows. When Athens carries off the treasure and tries to make vassals of its allies, the islands fight against Athens in allegiance to Sparta in the Peloponnesian War, which lasts 30 years. However, Náxos is subjugated and remains a tributary of Athens until the defeat of Athens. The outcome is a forever weakened Greece. Athens loses all importance.

Hellenistic Period (338–146 BC) The Macedonians in northern Greece take over Greek culture after conquering Greece in 338 BC. For a short period Alexander the Great, a Macedonian, takes this culture, henceforth known as "Hellenism", as far as India. After his early death his world empire rapidly disintegrates into Diadochean empires, the Aegean islands being dominated by the Egyptian Ptolemies. However the ideas of Hellenism, a cosmopolitan culture, continue to work their effect.

Roman Period (146 BC – 395 AD) After 146 BC the Romans, as the next rulers, also make Greek culture their own, thus helping it to spread throughout Europe. Greek culture becomes that of the Occident. Délos is now one of the wealthiest places in the Empire. From Rome comes Christianity, which also becomes the state religion in the Eastern Roman Empire after 391.

The Byzantine Period (395–1204 AD) The Roman Empire is divided in 395 AD. While the Western Roman Empire is in decline after the migration of peoples in 476 AD, the eastern part of the Imperium Romanum remains an upholder of Graeco-Roman culture for 1000 years. Byzantium, the second Rome, turns eastwards, brings Christianity to the Slavs and spreads Greek ideas as far as Moscow.
Especially on Náxos cruciform domed churches are built on the model of the Hagia Sophia in Constantinople. The new Islamic ideas also influence Greece in the 8th and 9th centuries. The iconoclastic controversy revolves around the admissibility of a pictorial representation of God and the Saints
㉒. The image worshipers prevail.
Europe begins to drift apart in cultural terms; the religious differences also deepen. The main points of dispute concern the Holy Ghost and the corporeal ascension of Mary. The popes dislike the fact that the Byzantine emperor is head of the church, while the Byzantines feel that Rome's reforms go too far. In 1054 the schism, or separation of the Eastern Greek-Orthodox Church from the Western Latin Church, comes about.
In these uncertain times the islands of the Aegean are often attacked by raiders such as the Vandals, the Goths, the Normans and finally the Saracens. The possibility of retreating into the in-

terior of the island and the huge refuge fort Apalírou make Náxos a relatively safer place, whereas the Small Cyklades are deserted for centuries. It isn't until the 9th century that Byzantium can consolidate its power once again.
However, in the wake of the Persians and Arabs, a new Asian power has assembled on the eastern borders of Byzantium: From 1071 the Turkmen Seljuks push westward. In 1095 the Eastern Roman Empire requests help from Pope Urban II, and the crusades begin. During the fourth crusade one of the most short-sighted campaigns in history is initiated. Due to trade rivalries Venice induces the crusaders to plunder and occupy the Byzantine capital, Constantinople, in 1204. The quadriga on San Marco square is part of the loot. Not until 1261 do the Byzantians conquer the city again with the aid of the Genoans, thus terminating the Venetians' "Latin Empire". Constantinople is too weak to ever recover again and is conquered by the Turks in 1453.

Venetian Era (1207–1537) For most of the Cycladic islands the domination of influential Venetian families begins after the sack of Constantinople. On Náxos the Sanudis and then the Crispis are the rulers of the Duchy of the Archipelago. They build fortified family seats, the pýrgi, and bolster Catholicism (p. 52). For 620 years foreign rulers now govern the island.

The Ottoman Era (1537–1827) The Fall of Constantinople in 1453 marks the end of the thousand-year-old advanced Roman-Greek civilisation. Learned Byzantine fugitives bring the Greek way of thinking back to the West again, paving the way for the Renaissance. From this time on the fortune of the Orthodox Church is determined in Moscow.
After the fall of Constantinople the Turkish-Ottoman Empire directs all its energy towards conquering Europe. After the fall of Rhodes in 1523, the Turks push on further west. In 1537 they conquer all the Cycladic islands apart from Tínos.
Yet in Greece itself the Ottoman influence, from diet to music, predominates for the next 350 years. This influence is still discernible today. Yet the islands partly enjoy greater freedom. The Turks are chiefly interested in obtaining revenue, even allowing the Jesuits to build a monastery ③. The Orthodox Church is recognised by the Turks as a mediator between government and population and proves to be the protector of Greek culture (p. 47).
Pan-Slavism under Catherine the Great seeks to bring the Balkan Slavs into the Russian fold. The Turkish-Russian war of 1768 to 1774 extends as far as the Aegean, where a Russian fleet occupies Náxos and 17 Cycladic islands for four years.

Independent Greece (since 1832) In 1821 the insurrection against the Turks begins on the Peloponnesus as Turkey has been weakened after another war against Russia. Europe reflects on its cultural roots. Philhellenists from many countries support the Greek struggle for independence, the Great Powers in Europe help diplomatically, and Greece becomes part of Europe again. In 1832 the rival great powers enthrone a "neutral" king, the Bavarian Otto I. From 1863 to 1975 the regents are then descended from the constitutional monarchy, a Danish-British dynasty.
From the end of the 19th century Greece tries to regain possession of its former settlements from the "sick man on the Bosporus". During the 1912–13 Balkan wars and the First World War several islands and Ottoman areas on the northern coast of the Aegean are occupied. After the First World War, among whose losers is Turkey, the opportunity appears favourable. The Greeks start a war over the former areas. But Turkey, emboldened once again by the "Young Turk Revolution", utterly destroys the Greeks, who then have to agree to a major population exchange. Over a million Greeks have to leave Asia Minor, where their ancestors had lived for 3,000 years.
In the 1930s Greece experiences a military dictatorship. In 1940 fascist Italy vainly attempts to occupy the country, whereupon German troops advance across the Balkans to Greece. They hand the country over to the Italians as conquered territory, but then occupy it themselves after Mussolini's fall in 1943. In October 1944, the Germans surrender to the British on Náxos.

After World War II With Western help during the civil war from 1945 to 1949, Greece avoids the fate of the other Balkan countries, and doesn't disappear behind the Iron Curtain.
After admission to the European Union, the latter's subsidies serve to improve the infrastructure and facilitate a growth in tourism, which becomes the most important economic sector in the country. The drachma, the oldest currency in the world, is replaced by the euro in 2002. The new, "hard" currency gives Greece easier access to financial resources, which many politicians are unable to resist. Unnoticed, huge mountains of debt are accumulated, which are used to service widespread clientelism. In the financial crisis after 2008 these debts can only be squared by extensive financial bailout measures on the part of the European Union. The economic reforms which the money lenders demand in return lead to social unrest and a new party landscape. The refugee crisis of 2015 also hits the country very badly. Although the problems have since eased somewhat, Greece still faces major challenges.

❶ The belvedere

The 5 to 6-hour hike on country lanes first leads past a solitary pebble beach. From there it climbs up to a belvedere above Naxos city and enjoys a fabulous view. The shadeless route has neither tavernas nor wells to offer.
■ 12 km, difference in altitude 270m, moderate

AWT 0.00 0.10 — You get off the morning bus to Engáres at **Galíni bus stop** on the main road. Follow a little street through Galíni in the direction of the sea. On the right you pass the **cemetery** and later greenhouses. Four minutes later you are annoyed by the barred gate which now blocks the way to

0.20 — Pýrgos Ypsilís (see below). But a minute later **two forks** lead uphill to the left.

> ***Alternative:*** If you continue along the little concrete road for a quarter of an hour, you reach the long **sandy beach of Amíti.**

0.20 0.30 — Take the fork over to the right (**P1:** N37°03.807'/E25° 29.833'), which runs across the **ridge** as a narrow concrete track and then heads towards two wind rotors. Be-

0.40 — low another **blocked drive** on the left stands the castle. As the neighbour is not too fussy about the fence, it is possible to catch a glimpse down on to the block-like pýrgos.

> *The Venetian **residential castle of Ypsilís** (14th century) has an inner courtyard with chapel. Two upper floors lean against the outside walls. Ghibelline battlements and a round tower can be seen. The enormous edifice later served as a monastery and is now in private ownership.*

0.45 — The level dirt track heads towards the **chapel** of Saint Paraskeví (**P2:** N37°07.852'/E25°25.115', 85m). To take a

1

2

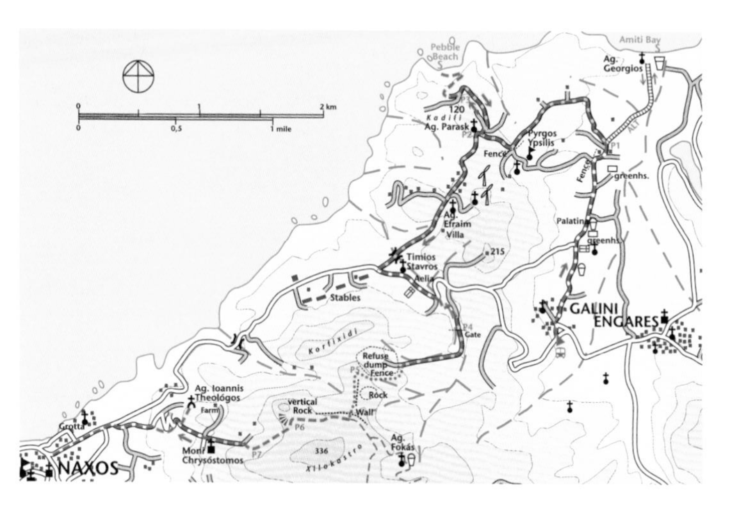

quick dip, descend right at the chapel through the barrier and later levelly towards the sea. After the lane takes a left bend, – before it rises – you leave it by going right on to a beautiful coastal path (**P3:** N37°08.046′/E25°25.017′). It

1.00 leads down to a deserted **pebble beach** 1 on the edge of the endless blue.

1.20 Return back up to the **Paraskeví Chapel** and right along the dirt track leading over the Kadíli hilltop. Passing a holiday home complex, you drop below the wind tur-

1.40 bines to the **road**, where you go left.

Walking past the Tímios Stavrós chapel (left), you skirt the cemetery (right), opposite which is situated the *Aelia*

1.45 artist's workshop. At the following **bridge** in the left bend in the dip you proceed straight ahead and find vestiges of a trail which run up from the valley to an asphalt road.

1.50 Further up you go through an open **gate** (**P4:** N37° 07.056′/E25°24.987′) and walk in the direction of the new landfill.

2.00 In front of the **fence** you ascend left without a path to the

2.10 **rocky outcrop** above the tip (**P5:** N37°06.811′/E25° 24.465′, 220m). To the left can be seen the marble quarries of Kinídaros. Cross a wide dip without a path, to the right of the rocks, alongside a wall 2. On the opposite slope, beneath Mount Xilókastro, you come to a somewhat indistinct path behind a long, transversal wall. Go right along this path towards an almost vertical boulder.

2.30 In the **saddle** to the left of it you are overwhelmed by the

3

4

view, which extends across the city as far as Páros 3 (**P6:** 37°06.611'/E25°24.081', 270m). The ideal place to take a well-earned early-evening break.

Proceed straight on downhill in the direction of the walls which run parallel to one another. In places it is necessary to avoid the overgrown trail by keeping left. Later the trail, sunken between fences on either side, runs towards a small holiday house (**P7:** N37°06.497'/ E25°23.820'), from where a steep concrete track leads down to the large

2.50 **Chrisóstomos Convent** 3. However, the building from the 17th/18th century is not accessible between 12.30 and 6.00 pm.

2.55 You walk down the road, taking care not to miss the **Grotto Chapel** of St. John 4 at the first bend up on the right. Here you can enjoy the sunset over the town and temple gateway, finishing up the last water rations in the process. Later you can shorten the loops in the road in order to

3.05 reach the **town** faster.

■ KTEL – PUBLIC BUSES

Bus journey times from Náxos town:
Chalkí 25, Filóti 30, Apíranthos 45 minutes, Kóronos 1hr., Koronída 1hr.20, Apóllonas (54 km) 1hr.45.

Timetables can be picked up at Chóra bus station. In May there are fewer buses.

Tickets are always sold near to bus stops – never by the bus driver! If you want to board a bus along the route, it is wise to have a ticket with you. Otherwise however the driver will also let one rectify the omission at the next point of sale. Prices e.g. € 2.30 Chóra – Chalkí.

❷ In the valley of the mills

Mostly on paths you ascend the fertile valley of Engarés to Kinídaros in 4 hours. Along the way are the ruins of seven typical watermills. Around Kinídaros you get to see the famous marble quarries.
🚌 Engarés, round trip to Artémios church.
■ 8 km, difference in altitude 395m, moderate

AWT 0.00 In the morning a minibus goes to **Engarés** (55m), where a marble block announces the trail "11" leading uphill. At the edge of the village it becomes a concrete track, running past a well (right) into a green valley. Later a group of
0.10 **house ruins** stands to the right of the path.
!! Opposite to where *the slight incline commences* an initially *indistinct path* forks left (**P1:** N37°03.420'/E25°30.571'). Later, on the left, is the **Pýrgos Brandoúnas**, an unoccupied Venetian nobleman's home from 1787. Ignore a right branch-off. For a while a water channel runs left alongside the path [1]. Through a wire-netting fence you
0.20 come to the stream at the first **mill** (**P2:** N37°06.914'/E25°26.838'). In the old Greek watermills the water plunged down through a pipe on to the mill wheel running horizontally below.

In the valley bottom lies a veritable jungle. Cross the stream and turn right past a motor pump. The stony path [2] forks in front of a fence. On the left trail "11A" leads up to the legendary cave where Diónysos was born, the present-day Jénnissis Chapel.

We drop right through the streambed and climb on the
0.25 right of an aqueduct up to a **roadway** (**P3:** N37°06.783'/E25°26.980'). Go left along it for a few meters and then continue along a path. Where this forks, go up right, at

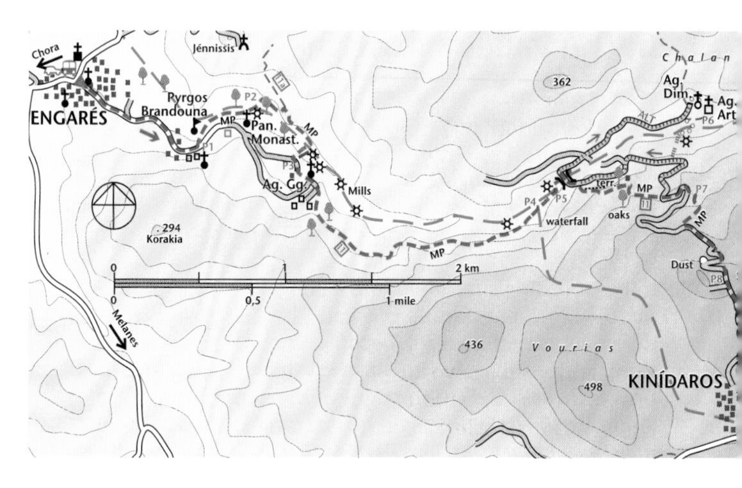

0.30 the next fork right again to the **St. George's Chapel** and on up to a roadway. Then left there, alongside ruins. Be-
!! fore the steepish incline be sure not to miss the *passage on*
0.45 *the left* to the next path! It leads through a little **forest.**
0.55 Later on the left runs the **watercourse** of another mill (**P4:** N37°06.538′/E25°27.874′, 160m). Again entering the rocky streambed, cross it on a dam in order to reach a
1.00 large **stone bridge.** It is easy to get on to on the far side (**P5:** N37°06.806′/ E25°28.028′, 325m).

Round trip: From the stone bridge a concrete track leads uphill and, in a quarter of an hour, to the ruin of the Byzantine Dimítros Chapel (right), part of a former monastery. Nestling below it is the triple-nave **Artémios Church** (18th century), for long the largest outside the city ③ (**P6:** N37°06.526′/ E25°28.143′). It is practically empty inside and usually locked.

Return by first going back along the roadway for 100m, but then after the fence down left without a path and through the streambed. Then 2 min. downstream and, behind a mill, up left to the roadway. Depending on your stamina, you can either ascend left there or quickly drop down to the bridge again.

1.00 On the normal route you cross the **stone bridge** and, after 50m, find stone slabs lying on the right above the gul-
1.05 ly. That is where the old trail begins, running above **olive terraces** and shortly afterwards through a little oak forest. The old paving stones can still be discerned in places. At the top you reach the roadway, which you proceed up for

1.20 two bends. 10m beyond the second one, a **right-hand bend**, the continuation of the old trail forks left (**P7:** N37°06.699'/E25°28.515', 315m). From the trail you can make out the large Artémios church in the valley. After about 7 min. you have to take the roadway again. In the concreted right bend you find, one meter higher up on the left, another section of the short-cut path. On the roadway again you encounter on the left, 60m beyond

1.35 the following right bend, the last stretch of **cobbled path** for today.

1.40 Back on the roadway you stride across a **saddle**, the highest point on the tour (**P8:** N37°06.405'/E25°28.690', 450m). The first view of the interior of the island opens up – with walled-in fields and marble mountains altered by human beings. The gigantic dimensions of the quarries can be better appreciated on the left as one descends [4].

At the fork in the road before the village you proceed left to the houses, only going right down the steps at a power

1.55 pole. Then left at an inn into the centre of **Kinídaros** with kafeníon and bus stop (departure about 3.15 pm).

■ Taxi

Telephone numbers: Chóra 0030-22850-22444/-24332 **Filóti** 6977-939321 · **Koronída** 6944-705863.

Prices from Chóra:
Engarés ca. 12 €, **Chalkí** 25 €, **Apíranthos** 37 €.

❸ The green valley of Potamiá

The magnificent circular hike from Melanés to "Kouros" bus station lasts just under 6 hours, so you should take a taxi to Melanés (about € 12) before 10 am.
Part of the route runs along one of the finest monopátia on Náxos. Nestling in the varied farmland with many olive groves are the ruins of a Catholic monastery and the ancient marble quarry of Flério with two large, half-finished marble statues. A shady garden inn and several wells are also to be found.
Taking the bus already at Koúros is a way of shortening the walk.
🚗 Melanés
■ 10 km, difference in altitude 150m, moderate

AWT 0.00 — To the right of the "Agkor" taverna at the **bus stop in Melanés** you enter the village alley and after 3½ min., to the right of the "Vasilis" taverna, go up the steps – eagerly eyed by huge colourful roosters. The village, which only has 500 inhabitants, boasts many inns specializing in chicken and rabbit dishes. At the end of the village you

0.05 — come to a **bend in the road** and go up right. Down on the left stands the new church. Rising above are ornate terraces, in spring covered in luscious green [1].

After three minutes you turn left into a country lane and, after a further five minutes, *on the same level,* left again at

0.15 — a fork. At the immediately following **fork** with the signposts (**P1:** N37°05.011'/E25°26.307') you proceed right and, after 100m, down right at the next sign. You walk past a coop (right, hens of course) and march down to the valley alongside an olive grove. Round a bend you suddenly see a large building [2] below the roadway. Hesitant-

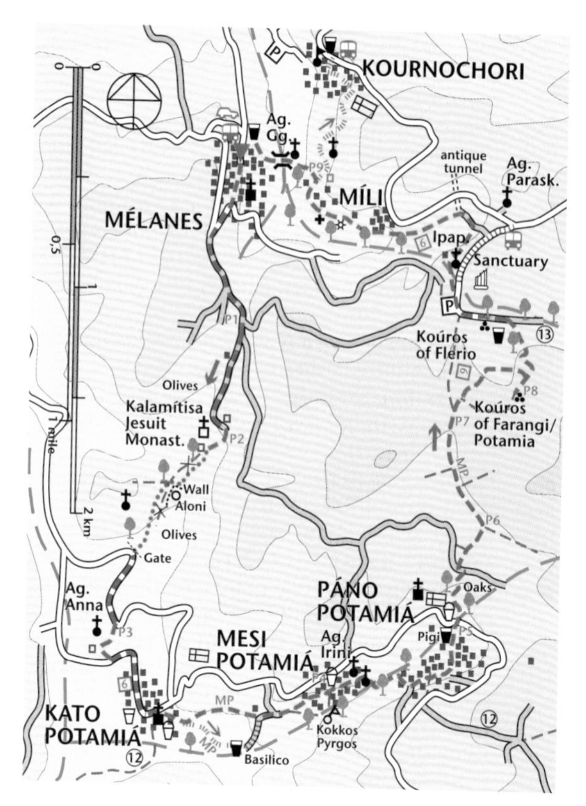

0.25 ly you enter the ruins of the **Jesuit Monastery Kalamítsia** (**P2:** N 37°04.745/E25°26.260', 135m).

From the 17th century, on what was then Osman Náxos, the Jesuits ran a monastery and large estates. Their commercial success led to tensions with the local farmers. Travellers were always welcome as guests of the monastery that existed until 1927.

Today one first enters the tall refectory, with reception rooms on either side. The monastic cells are in the lower building at the back.

In the prolongation of the country lane there is a clear path for hikers above the overgrown trail. Later, at a low wall with a gap, is a scarcely discernible **fork.** Here you do *not go through the gap* into the raised field (with threshing area), but a few meters to the right and immediately left on to a monopáti. Because this soon becomes overgrown,

0.30 !!

it is best to walk parallel with it on the right. Further down well-beaten paths run through an olive grove to the

0.35 **road.** There we go through a gate and up left, but only for four minutes! In the first sharp left-hand bend we leave the road at the traffic mirror (**P3:** N37°04.239′/ E25°25.928′, 90m) and go right, alongside the fence of the old Anna Chapel, and down a mule track. Then, further down at some ruins, left down to a concrete track "6" and

0.50 left up this to the large church of **Káto Potamiá** (85m). Below it lies the nice garden inn of a hobby innkeeper. Then we follow a lane up the valley for three minutes as far as a fork above a rectangular manhole cover.

> ***Alternative:*** Walking downhill one comes to the garden inn *"Basiliko"* and the ruin of the Kokkos Pýrgos (see p. 58). At AWT 1.05 one returns to the main route (see below).

★ Climbing up to the left, we find a beautiful old mule track

1.00 lined by walls. A short way along a **road**, then straight

1.05 ahead at the steps (right) and up. On the left in **Mési Potamiá** is a well. (**P4:** N37°04,080′/E25°26,594′, 180m). This is where we are rejoined by the alternative route.

At the end of the village a paved roadway leads up left to the Iríni chapel. At the top we turn immediately to the

1.10 right, past a small **chapel** with an overlapping stone slab roof (right), into the valley half hidden by trees (left).

Proceeding along the shady stream, we climb up to the

!! right after 80m at a spring until *facing* old stone steps in the continuation of the path. Here we walk left on the level, along the main alley in **Páno Potamiá** (Odos Giampoúra) as far as the Platía Orphanoú – really just a widening of the street. (On the right steps lead to Chalkí.) Continue straight on, then down. On the left at the well

1.20 lies the popular **garden inn *"Pigí"***, the source. In case anyone has overlooked it: **P5:** N37°04.209′/E25°26.981′, 170m.

Leaving the garden, we head straight on, to the right of the source, car park and church, in to the narrow alley leading up to the road, which we cross (sign "Flerio"). Directly at the cemetery (left), beneath oaks, begins one of

★ the most beautiful mule tracks on Náxos ③. Although traversed by a concrete track, it continues, displaced 20m to

1.30 the left. The path reaches a **fork** (**P6:** N37°04.512′/ E25°27.049′). Here we follow the sign "Kouros" to the left. Above a dip we saunter gaily between olive trees, ignoring two branch-offs, as far as the highest point of the hike at

245m. Some distance away on the right we can make out
1.40 the quarried marble mountains of Kinídaros. At a **fork** (**P7:** N37°04.789'/E25°26.987') we go right along a narrow, overgrown path. Behind a gap in the wall we cross a paved track and stand in a small archaeological park – a marble quarry in antiquity. Up until some years ago the
1.50 **Koúros of Farangi** (or Potamiá) lay hidden between the bushes (see p. 62 4) – the privilege of seeing it without GPS was not granted to many (**P8:** N37°04.866'/E25° 27.235').

"Kouroi" are larger-than-life ancient sculptures of standing youths. The two on today's hike were destined for shrines, but were never finished due to material defects. The female counterpart is called a "kore".

The cobbled path leads down to the dry-bed and there to the left. At the second gap in the wall, 40m further down,
2.00 can be found the other sculpture, the **Koúros of Flério** 4. And beside it a modest garden inn.

Back on the concrete track, we walk left and, before the car park in the dip, up to the right – a cobbled path commences after about 50m.

It is possible to walk up the road to the right and visit the new archaeological excavation of the ***shrine of the stonemasons.*** *This is a round site with a diameter of forty metres which was dedicated to a goddess of fertility, whose two sons were the patron saints of the stonemasons. During antiquity this shrine belonged to the quarry. Further up, you can catch the bus home at 3.15 pm.*

If one takes the said cobbled path "6" to the left along the
2.05 slope, one soon comes below **Ipapánti Chapel.** After a section fit for traffic, a path branches off to the right further down.

Beneath a canopy lies the entrance to a 220m long tunnel

from the 6th century BC. It was part of the 11 km long ancient water pipeline from the rainy Flério plain to the ancient city.

The path plunges into the green valley, where huge cactus figs form a guard of honour. Below the houses in **Míli** one strolls on and drops down left in front of a house blocking the way. Standing in the gardens on the left are three old water mills. Here our wall-lined path is accompanied by a gully. Next comes a **wayside altar** on the left. Keep straight ahead on the same level. After the last houses in Míli (left, with external staircase) begins the narrow stepped path down into the valley (**P9:** N37°05.302'/ E25°26.538', 160m).

2.20

> ***Alternative:*** Continuing on would bring you to **Kournochóri** with the Venetian Frangópolis castle residence. Up on the road you could also catch a bus shortly before 3.00 pm.

In the valley, where the descent from Milí ends, stands the closed St. George's chapel; the 1,500-year history of this edifice does not show. On the other side of the valley we head up to **Melanés**, where our hire car is waiting or the **bus** appears at about 2.45 pm.

2.35
2.40

④ To the dunes of Pláka

From Vívlos we take an attractive, 2½-hour downhill trail to the fertile coastal plain and wander through the fields to the extensive sand dunes of Pláka.
■ 6 km, difference in altitude 150m, easy

AWT 0.00 From the bus top in **Vívlos**, aka **Trípodes**, we set off slightly uphill past inns (left) and the chemist's shop (right). Having passed a flight of steps (left), we go down the signposted alley on the right. Then left to the Platía and straight on in the same direction.

0.05 In the **rift-valley** on the southern perimeter of the village, below a large church with several towers, a roadway leads us along the upper edge of the wide valley to two chapels. The first one, enclosed by a fence, is on our left

0.20 as we proceed. Before the second, **St. George's Chapel** (150 m) [1] (beautiful icons), we turn left below the rock with the ruin of a watchtower and, after 60m, down right. At the hollow the roadway runs past another chapel (right), to the right and then uphill. Lying between the

0.25 rocks is the **grotto chapel Agios Nikoláos** (**P1:** N37° 03.069′/E 25°23.900′, 125m). From the broad path leading down to the sea we have a commanding view of the coastal plain. Spread out on the right is the plain of Pláka, lush farmland with plentiful water supplies. Wine, cereals and vegetables are cultivated, but above all potatoes, a culinary delight much relished by Greek connoisseurs.

0.35 Down in the **plain of Pláka** (**P2:** N37°03.080′/E25° 23.555′) we keep to the right and encounter reed-covered paths (see p. 11 [1]), which eventually lead right to a little

0.45 **concrete road** running at right angles (**P3:** 37°03.169′/ E25°23.188′).

1

2

If you follow it 250m to the right, you come to the ruins of the Paléopýrgos, a Hellenic fortress-tower made of dry cut stone. These fortified rural residences were wide-spread in the Aegean. The tower with five to seven floors and the wall thickness of one metre afforded protection against assault.

Heading towards the sea, we then walk past two rocky hills (right) and the St. Matthew's chapel 2 (left, with an-

0.55 cient structural parts). The sandy track runs on to the **asphalt road.** There we dash right for 150m and turn off left on to a roadway in front of the holiday studios. This brings us to the Sea Melody hotel complex and the infi-

1.10 nite **dune beach of Pláka.**

Our hike is crowned by a barefoot trek alongside the

1.20 sandy beach to the **bus stop** at the *Plaza Hotel*. Or 5 min. further to the shady beach inn *"Petrino"*, likewise with a bus connection. Or even further along the dunes ...

Information on the internet

The website *www.ucke.de/christian/naxos* provides special information on Náxos. The owner, Munich physicist **Christian Ucke**, wrote the first hiking book on Náxos in 1984 (downloadable on the site). Together with Dieter Graf, he published an extended version in 2003. His rich knowledge of Náxos has also been incorporated into this new book.

⑤ The re-erected temple

This 4½-hour trek leads you through a charming landscape past the re-erected Temple of Demeter and on along lanes over a plateau with tilled fields. Finally you come to the long sandy beach of Pláka. That is your first chance to take a rest in a taverna.
Ano Sangrí, two possible round trips back to the car.
■ 11 km, difference in altitude 220m, moderate

AWT 0.00 We jump off the bus at the **Ano Sangrí junction** and march 500m along the road to the village. Turning half-right at the crossroads before it, we bear left of the monument in the small pine wood, down to the concrete road. There left for 150m and left again along a village alley

0.10 to the uninhabited monastery **Ayios Eleftérios**, now a museum.

Beside the monastery, to the right of a stone gentleman with a bow-tie, we descend the steps and wander to the right on a country lane in the direction of a hill chapel. Later the lane runs along below the chapel [1]. On the left you later see a wide plain with olive trees and, opposite at an angle, the temple [2] on the hill. Our lane leads above a

0.20 **farm shed (P1:** N37°02.101'/E25°26.056') and becomes a mule track. Later we drop down along a well-beaten track on the left into the hollow, go right, then left and, on the track leading towards the middle of the valley, through the dry-bed. Secret paths bring us to the museum of the

0.30 **temple.**

*The **Temple of Demeter** from 530 BC measured 12.6 x 13.2m and consisted completely of marble except for two wooden doors. The cella had no windows and bare walls – thus creating the atmosphere of a cave when the doors*

1

2

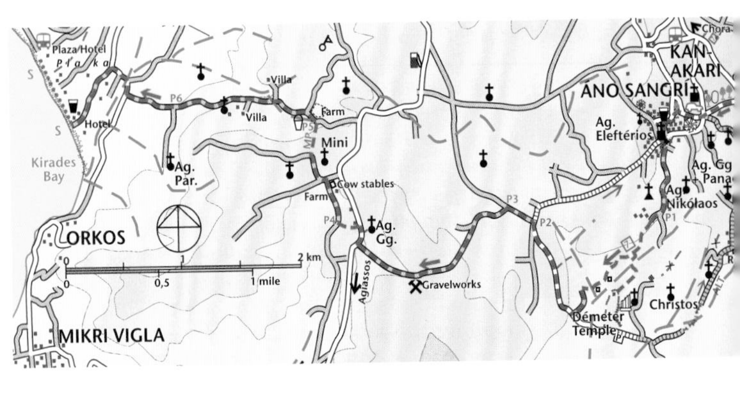

were closed. However the roof was covered with just 2-4 cm thick, translucent marble tiles. This suggests that nocturnal celebrations were held here in honour of the goddess of fertility Demeter until the first daylight became perceptible through the ceiling.
In the floor in front of the temple can be seen the foundations of the extensions from 500 AD (p. 38).

Round trip: From the temple down to the parking bay, there left and after 250m left again on to the second country lane.

Taking the road hardly saves any time, so we return to the original path, traverse the hollow again, come to the already familiar monopáti and go left. On our left is the re-erected temple and we take pleasure in the fact that an ancient temple has again become part of this delightful landscape. A ruined house provides a suitable picnic spot. ★

0.40 We then trudge on through a **hollow**, which is sometimes wet in spring, and up the lane to the road, where we head

3

4

0.50 right in a northerly direction. At the **crossing** (sign in the opposite direction: Dímitras, **P2:** N37°02.032'/E25°25.335', 170m) the route leads straight on along a country lane. (Drivers bear right to return to Ano Sangrí.)

We are surrounded by wide fields and solitary, shady trees which have been severely punished by the wind. Now

0.55 turn left at the **fork** (**P3:** N37°02.140'/E25°25.104'), left again at a second fork and over the hill (225m) which marks the boundary of the plain. On the way down, the track passes a gravel/cement works (left) and ends at the

1.20 **road.**

We have to march 100m along it to the right, until we are below the chapel Ágios Geórgios on the slope (right) 3. There on the left beside the road stands a three-storey house; along its lower fence we stalk cross-country for

1.25 120m and hit upon a **country lane** (**P4:** N37°02.115'/E25°24.162') in the hollow. Walk up it to the right as far as cattle sheds (right) and walls blocking your path, go left

1.30 and then right in front of a **farmhouse.** A little farther on you must watch out: about 30m to the right of the road-

1.35 way stands a **miniature barrel-vaulted chapel** with free-standing bell-tower.

!! At the left-hand bend we go *straight ahead* and immediately find a rather overgrown, yet negotiable mule track; keep to its left edge. After 200m, beside a pasture, it meets

1.40 a **roadway**, which we take to the left (**P5:** N37°02.519'/E25°24.042', 130m). Shortly afterwards we stumble across a well on the left.

The way now leads through quiet countryside 4 towards

1.50 the sea. At the **fork** beside a power pole with transformer we go left and come past several new villas.

2.00 Down on the **coastal plain** a roadway branches off to the left (**P6:** N37°02.579'/E25°23.160') – we ignore it and come to the road. We go right, then left, then not into the

2.10 cul-de-sac, but follow the **sign "Beach".** What a relief to dispose of those garments!

2.25 We tramp along the strand until reaching the **bus stop** *"Plaza Hotel"*. Further stops follow.

Temples on Náxos

Besides Délos and Páros, the only important temples of the Greek Classical Period in the Cyclades can be found on Náxos. Here, three temples have been excavated and examined.

The **Temple to Apóllon** on the Palátia peninsula in front of the city (p. 4). Around 530 BC the tyrant Lýgdamis started building the temple, but after his fall it was never completed. With exterior measurements of 24 x 55m and a pillar height of about 13m, it would have become one of the largest temples of those days.
Distributed across several islands were a total of 22 Apollo shrines of different sizes which were oriented towards the holy island of Délos. From them came light signals on the occasion of the major annual festivals in honour of the Délian League.
1000 years later the temple was transformed into an early-Christian basilica and a further 800 years later it was used as a quarry for the Chóra by the Venetians.

The **Temple to Demeter in Sangrí** (p. 33) from the same period was discovered in 1949 on account of the noticeably large number of architectural fragments in the at that time isolated chapel of Saint John. Later excavations proved the uniqueness of this rural Ionic temple which, structurally, is regarded as a precursor of the Parthenon Temple in Athens.
The tremendous accomplishment of archaeologists and architects consisted in being able to visualise the ancient temple among approximately 1600 fragments scattered all over, some of which had even been built into the walls of farmhouses. Then the chapel of Saint John was taken apart and moved aside, and the temple was put together as a puzzle with 40% of the original marble fragments and the rest new. This took five years until 2001.
Laid open in the ground in front of the temple are the foundations of the apse and monastery of the extensions and conversions from 500 AD to the early-Christian, three-aisle basilica (p. 38).

The approximate site of **the Temple to Diónysos of Iría,** south of the city, had been known from reports. After intensive questioning of some of the farmers in the fields, the right spot could be located in 1986. Excavations revealed four levels of temples exactly axially on top of each other. The lowest one from the 8th century BC had a width of only five metres. The 300 year younger and most recent, the upper level, had measurements of 13 x 29m. The excavation field has now been covered again and secured. It is only accessible at irregular times.

⑥ Byzantine chapels

This 3 to 4-hour round trip through farming country which, on account of the numerous Byzantine chapels, is sometimes referred to as "Little Mistras". It also takes in the Demeter Temple, in the Byzantine era a basilica. The green undulating plain has no wells to offer, but Ano Sangrí has two tavernas.
Ano Sagrí
■ ***8 km, difference in altitude 100m, easy***

AWT From the **bus stop in Ano Sangrí** it is 500m to the cross-
0.00 roads before the village. On the right is the sports field.
0.05 Diagonally opposite the bus shelter at the **crossing** our country lane leads down left. Embedded in the mountains on the left you can see the village of Moní. 400m be-
0.10 yond a **farmhouse** with "pasture" (left) the old Byzantine
0.15 double church **Ágios Georgios & Panagía** comes into view on the right 1. It contains frescoes from the 11th to 13th centuries, but is unfortunately closed.
Continuing straight ahead on the lane, we behold the fertile plain of Sangrí ahead of us. Ignore a branch-off to the right (**P1:** N37°02.078'/E25°26.474') and climb slightly.
0.20 At a fork in front of a **ruined house** we bear right and, 200m further (120m before the white Dimitri chapel),
!! *turn at an acute angle down right* on to a **narrow lane**
0.25 (**P2:** N37°01.906'/E25°26.377', 165m).
In the walled streambed we go left for a bit, then half right uphill and through an olive grove without a path. 50 meters above the streambed (left) traces of a path run to the right of a fence. From here we can now see the chapel 2, which is very quickly reached (**P3:** N37°
0.30 01.772'/E25°26.124'). The **Christós cross-domed chapel**

1

2

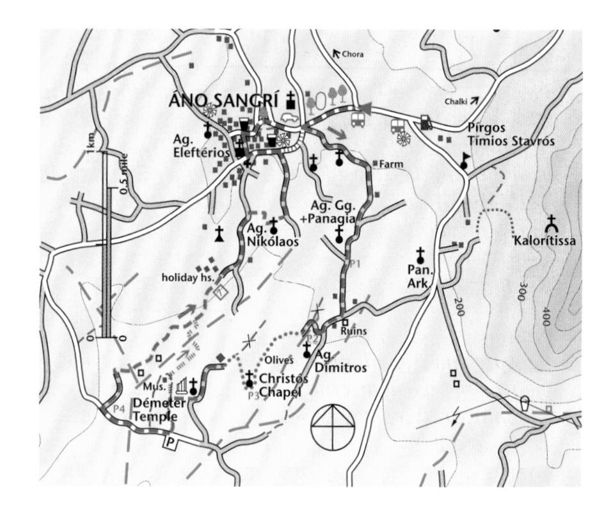

possesses the remains of frescoes of saints in the bema, the altar room.

On the side with the entrance a wide doorway opens on to a picnic place beneath an olive tree. Quite a few of ★ these gnarled old trees stand in the meadow across which, past a bell in a tree, we subsequently tramp uphill without a path. At the top our way is crossed by an overgrown monopáti, turns off to the left beside it and passes a new

0.35 **shed**. Behind this we follow the ruts until, all of a sudden, we find ourselves standing in front of a dappled temple ③. The lighter marble slabs date from the reconstruction of 2001.

0.40 *The ancient **Démeter Temple** was converted into a three-aisled **early Christian basilica** around 500 AD. At that time the western outer wall of the temple was replaced by inner columns and the column porch enclosed. The direction of the roof ridge was turned by 90° and an*

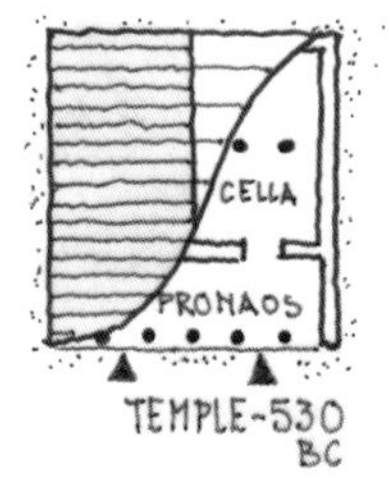

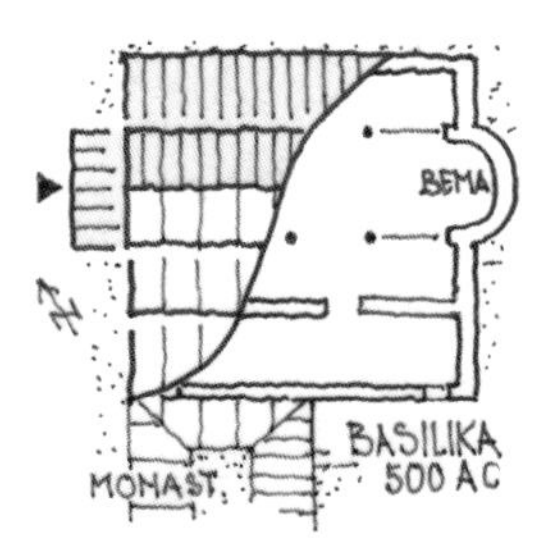

apse and a small monastery attached to the outside. This was the religious centre of the whole region at that time.
Shortcut: The way through the dip below the museum is described on p. 33.

To be able to take in the wonderful position of the former temple, though, one ought to ramble round it after the visit. To do so, descend the footpath to the parking bay and walk right on the road. After six minutes a country lane (**P4:** N37°01.706'/E25°25.575') takes you to the right through a dip, which however is often damp in spring. There you reach a beautiful footpath 4, which reveals the exalted position of the temple on the right. A little later a

1.05 **monopáti** leads down right – the shortcut described above. But you go straight on and come on to a country

1.10 lane which climbs left next to a **small shed** (right).

1.15 Below the first houses in Ano Sangrí you go down a **defile** to the right. It leads to the (closed) Byzantine cross-domed church Ágios Nikoláos. It houses frescoes from the 11th century AD and affords a final view across the countryside, which Byzantinologists have compared with Mistras and its numerous chapels on the Peloponnese. Staying on the path, you discover a lane, which takes you

1.25 uphill to the **windmills** of **Áno Sangrí** with café.

Going right here would bring you to the bus stop in 6 min.

Going left leads to the Eleftérios monastery. The alley before it runs right to the road with "Johnnys" garden taverna. Steps run up to a small pine copse and on to the cross-

1.35 roads and 500m further to the **bus stop** on the main road.

7 Beachcombers

The tranquil 2 to 3-hour beach hike offers various destinations. First it shows the farming hinterland with the typical reed walls. Then, walking along the long sandy beach, it passes a very nice taverna in Kastráki.
There one has to decide whether to shuffle back or press on to the Agáli peninsula. Shade is scarce!
Mikrí Vígla or Kastráki
■ *8 km to Agáli, easy*

AWT 0.00 The bus drops us off at **Mikrí Vígla** rock, the highest point for miles around. At the usually dry saltwater lake we want to start by heading inland on a roadway. Half way along the "lake" we leave the road and proceed "on the lake" to the right, shortly afterwards inland and through the Lianos Studios.

At the rear entrance we stroll straight ahead as far as a transversal country lane. There we go right, and again at a

0.10 **shed** (right) (**P1:** N37°01.295'/E25°22.821'). We are surrounded by corn fields, which are later protected against erosion by three metre high reed walls [1]. Corn and the popular Naxos potatoes are cultivated here, some livestock also graze in this labyrinth.

At an electricity substation are two side entrances to fields. Our lane ends in front of a reed wall, however it is

0.20 possible to squeeze through a **gap** with hose and grating (**P2:** N37°01.099'/E25°22.763'). Now we proceed straight ahead across the open field, left for a few metres in front of the next reed wall and right at the "corner". After 100m we go straight ahead across the traversal country lane.

Shortly afterwards, on the right, are a metal gate and an

0.25 elongated shed, then again on the right stands a **cottage**

1

2

(**P3:** N37°00.985'/E25° 22.868'). Here we turn off right and saunter alongside a vineyard (right) towards the sea. After a dilapidated fence and wheel ruts we

0.30 are back on sandy **Sahara Beach.**

Now comes the most wonderful stretch of beach, although shady tamarisks are not to be found until (in the mornings) at the small **Kastráki** bay between solitary, flat rocks. A little further on, however, the roof of the nice

0.45 **beach taverna *"Paradise"*** affords more shade. In front of it is the bus stop – should one wish to stay longer …

An initially shady roadway leads south alongside holiday houses to

1.05 **Glifáda**. There we reach a large inn, set back somewhat from the sea, and another dry lake. The bus stops 100m inland on the main road. Should one care to wander on, one encounters more beach goers – but at least the houses are further away ②. On Agáli peninsula, towards which one heads, no development can be discerned. A rare species of elder bush grows there, which ex-

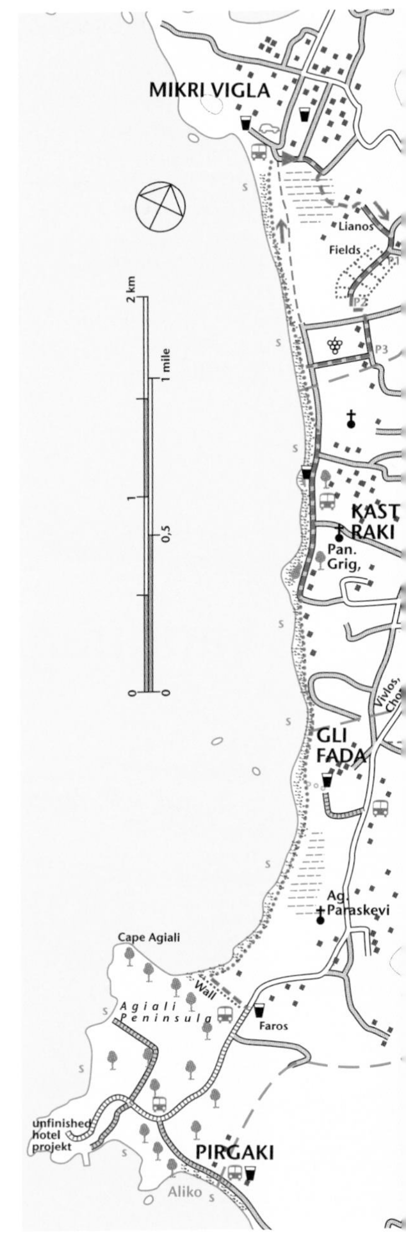

plains why the peninsula is to be declared a conservation area.
In front of the bushes we follow the stone wall up left and arrive at the sizeable road-house, *"Faros"*, directly on the
1.25 **road.** Here we could catch the **bus** at about 18.05.
From here the route to **Agáli** peninsula runs on asphalt for 10 min. as far as a *right bend* (**P4:** N36°58.831'/ E25°23.492', bus stop) and a further 5 min. to the right and the ruins of a hotel complex. We are rewarded by two
1.40 very beautiful **bathing bays.**

From the *right bend* a dusty track leads *left* down to **Pirgáki**, with bus stop and taverna.
And marvellously fine sand – "Psilí Ámmos" in Greek.

❽ The Byzantine Apalírou Castle

The 5½-hour tour leads along country lanes on the perimeter of a wide plain and then steeply up to the ruins of the enormous Byzantine castle on the 474m high Apalírou. On top there is no path between the rocks, where one should be sure-footed.
One comes across a well.
road to Agiassós
■ 10 km, difference in altitude 250m, moderate to difficult

AWT
0.00 On the bus to Chalkí ask the driver to stop at the **branch-off to Agiassós**, aka **Bazéos.** On the rear side of the petrol station walk up beside the windmills (right) until you
0.05 come to **Pýrgos Bazéos** [1].

The name recalls the owners in the 19th century; the equally common name Tímios Stavrós ("true cross") recalls the earlier times when it was a monastery. It was originally built as a refuge castle in the period of the pirate raids. Inside are a church with dome and frescoes from the 12th century.

Continuing along the road, one could take the roadway climbing left after 150m and visit the cave church Kalóritsa. It is situated beneath the ruins one can spot beneath
0.12 the rocks (p. 47). At the second **branch-off**, in a slight right-hand bend (**P1:** N37°02.127'/E25°26.883,), you leave the road to the left and take an initially ascending country lane. In your walking direction appears a towering, cone-shaped mountain. Our destination, oh dear! [2]
0.20 After passing a few **house ruins** (right), we are joined by a power line. To the right a wide plain extends as far as the
0.25 sea. Then, down on the right, is a **pump**, a second one (left) later offers a water tap.

20m beyond the pumping station we take the path on the right through the gully and right again up the country lane. After a wide gate the vehicle tracks pass through tall juniper bushes and end near some sheds. Beyond a gate with vertical closure rod a path leads us on between these, curving

0.40 to the left after more **ruins.** Running beside a fence (right), it ends at a walled-in grove (**P2:** N37°01.181′/ E25°27.137, 180m). From there a country lane takes us right. At a VW-van-cum-chicken-shack we turn up left and come to a small

0.50 **farmhouse.**

Up on the left a proud sign marks the beginning of the path to the kástro. But one should not try too hard to find this: it only consists of goat tracks. Go up the path, keeping to the right. Further up, stay about 100m to the left above a saddle where, after traversing the crest, you

1.10 come to a **path** which is little easier to follow (**P3:** N37°00.774′/E25°27.049′) through scree to the right and

1.35 later reaching the defence wall of **Kástro Apalírou** 3.

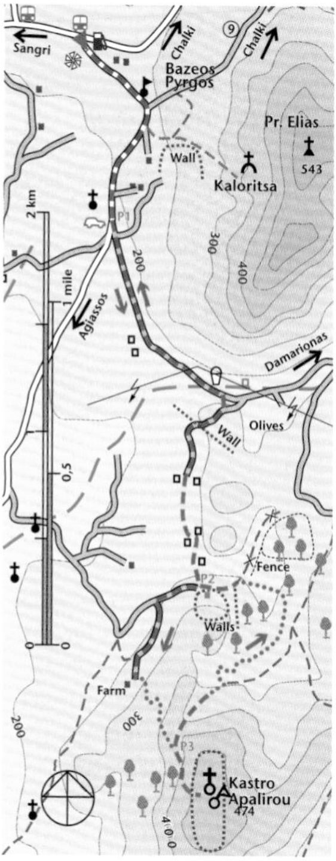

The kástro was the island's main fortress at least from the 8th century. After the Byzantines were ejected by the Genoese, the latter had to defend themselves against the Venetians in 1207. Following a five-month siege Marco Sanudo became ruler of Náxos. He built his own castle, the Apáno Kástro, and left this edifice to decay.

The castle's field of ruins has the gigantic dimensions of 350 x 50 to 90 metres. The position of the doorways is not known. Only a small part of the defence wall is left, it is easier to make out the remains of a few defence towers. In the ruins of the actual building it is easiest to recognize the cisterns, smoothed inside with reddish, clayey plaster.

The chapel is from a later date. The view across the island is extremely rewarding.

1.35 To descend, use the familiar path, which later (at **P3**) swings right to the north-east into the cultivated dip. It
2.10 peters out a little further down – not until on the **valley floor** do you find more recognizable tracks again ④. Having passed the first round hill on the left, you see walls on the left in front of the next hill. Sticking to its right-hand side, you proceed through a gate on to a monopáti and, on the left, find your way back to the walled-in grove (**P2**). From there you stroll right, along the already famil-
2.45 iar trail back to the **pumping station**.
The wide roadway on the right is not very attractive. Better go left along the familiar lane and later the road to the
3.10 **bus stop.**

⑨ In the plain of Tragéa

A 2½-hour trek to whet your appetite, through fields and olive groves and along easily identifiable tracks and paths with a pleasant stop at a taverna in Chalkí, the heart of the Tragéa plateau. With a visit to the imposing Kalorítsa cave church it lasts one hour longer.
Agiassos turning, by bus back to the car
■ *6 km, difference in altitude 60m, easy*

AWT
0.00 Just after the Áno Sangrí bus stop you alight at the **turning to Agiassós** (aka Baséou). Here you head up along the road between the petrol station and the windmills (right),
0.05 to the bulky, unadorned **Pýrgos Bazéou** (also called **Pýrgos Tímios Stavrós** i.e. "true cross"). The medieval fortified monastery has been converted into the region's cultural centre (p.43).

Detour to the cave church: You go down the road and, after 150m, 20m before the roadway, turn left on to a footpath, which is difficult to make out at first. Further up it runs immediately to the left of the field wall and in 18 min. leads up to a few isolated ruins in the rocks. Below them (**P1:** N36°58.020'/E24°42.072') you discover the Kalorítsa Cave Church, the "propitious Mother of God" [1], whose history goes back to the 4th century BC. From above it is possible to look in to the closed church, which houses very valuable mural paintings [1]. During Turkish rule it was a secret school, in which the children were taught religion and the Greek alphabet by monks.

You descend on the same path, but turn right near the farm on to a level path. Above the Pýrgos Baséou you come across a roadway and go right.

1

2

0.05 Directly behind the **Pýrgos Bazéou** a roadway ascends over slabs of rock in to the olive groves. At the left turn
0.10 you go right and past a **water cistern** (right).
The track is lined by nut bushes and olive trees. Disregarding several turnings to the right, wander straight down in
0.20 to the **hollow**, where you come across an attractive paved stone path through a field (**P2:** N37°02.719'/E25°27.499', 265m). Bear right ahead of the fence on wheel ruts, down in to the already familiar shady lane and walk left. From a
0.25 **small hill** you look across the beautiful plain of Tragéa, which remains green all year.
The torso of a windmill is visible left on a hill; we march on unwaveringly below it, on what is now a concrete
0.30 track which makes a **left-hand bend** – at this very spot we take the second path to the right up to the small church **Agios Nektários** on the hilltop 2.
While descending, we are taken aback by the two industrial buildings, but can avoid them by keeping right on a somewhat tangly path. After the bridge stroll by the chapel for 50m further on and bear left on to a roadway lined by gnarled olive trees (**P3:** N37°03.293'/E25°004').
0.40 Then later, at the **fork** after the Byzantine Taxiarchis Chapel (right, with non-iconic frescoes), we naturally take the more attractive path down right into a dry-bed,
0.50 right there for 30m before going up a few steps to **Chímarros** and right to the road.
Head uphill past the cemetery (right), turn right at the
0.55 washing area at the small church of **Tsikalarió** before heading down again, contentedly, over a splendidly shady paved path and left on the roadway below.
You take this roadway for only 50m and turn down right through the dry-bed at some markings (**P4:** N37°03.838'/E25°28.580'). On the other side is a sunken path leading to Chalkí.

From a three-way junction one could follow the signs left before the edge of the village and, in five minutes, reach the beautiful church **Agios Geórgios o Diassorítis** (George the Rescuer), an example of a Byzantine cruciform-domed church with valuable frescoes inside. In July and August open from 11 a.m. to 1 p.m.

Keeping right at the first houses in **Chalkí** (290m), we
1.15 take a look at the **platía** to see who else is lolling around in front of Giannis' taverna.
Later on, you can get the bus at the church of Protótronis with its superb interior.

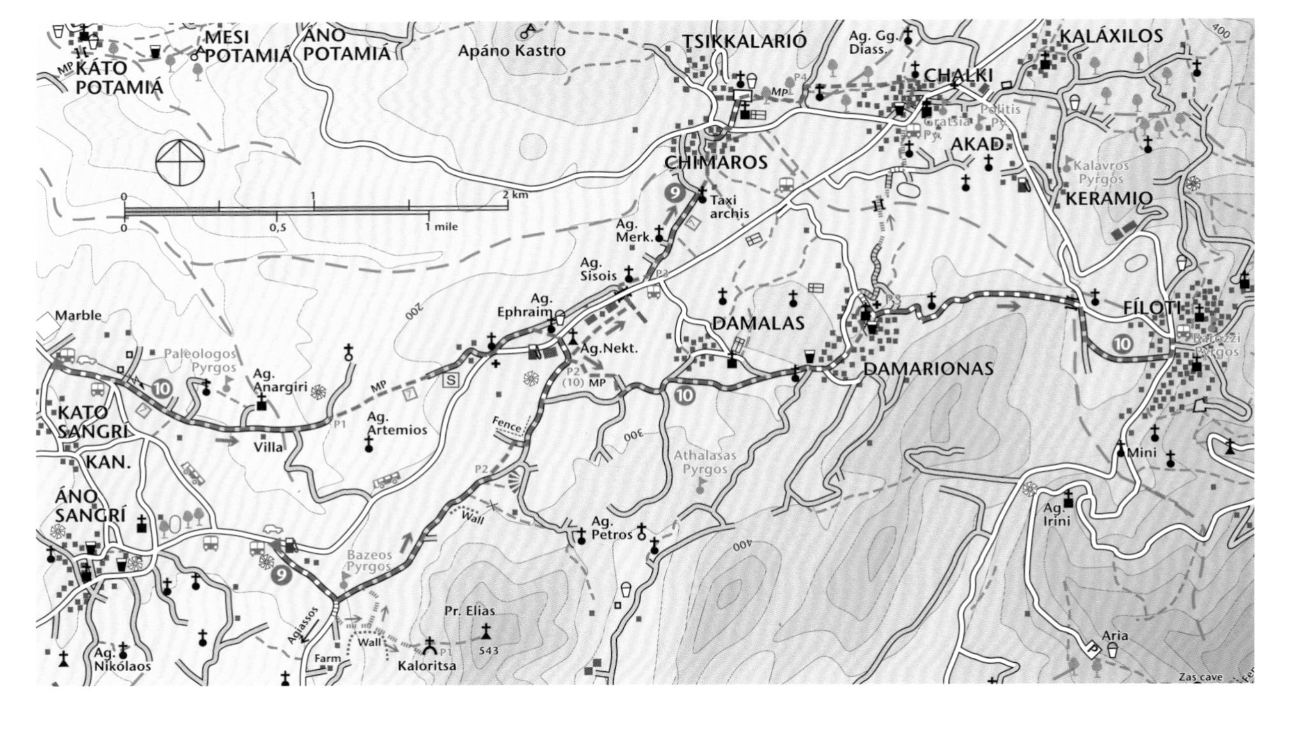
MESI POTAMIÁ
ÁNO POTAMIÁ
KÁTO POTAMIÁ
Apáno Kastro
TSIKKALARIÓ
Ag. Gg. Diass.
CHALKI
KALÁXILOS
Politis Py.
Gratsia Py.
AKAD.
Kalavros Pyrgos
KERAMIO
CHIMAROS
Taxi archis
0
1
2 km
0,5
1 mile
Ag. Merk.
Ag. Sisois
Ag. Ephraim
Ag.Nekt.
DAMALAS
FÍLOTI
Barozzi Pyrgos
DAMARIONAS
Marble
Paleologos Pyrgos
Ag. Anargiri
Ag. Artemios
KATO SANGRI
Villa
KAN.
ÁNO SANGRÍ
Fence
200
300
400
Athalasas Pyrgos
Mini
Ag. Irini
Wall
Ag. Petros
Bazeos Pyrgos
Pr. Elias
543
Agiassos
Farm
Kaloritsa
Ag. Nikólaos
Aria
Zas cave

⑩ Venetian pýrgi

A 3-hour trek through Arcadian landscapes to Filóti or Chalkí. Walk along the old main path through the island, protected by ancient tower-houses or pýrgi. These medieval fortress-towers were the easily defensible country residences of the Venetian nobility (see below).
🚗 Káto Sangrí, bus back to the car
■ 9 km, altitude difference 160m, easy to moderate
▷ map see previous page

AWT It's best to tell the bus driver where you want to get off shortly before you get there, i.e. **Káto** (lower) **Sangrí.** (There is a marble factory on the left, just before the road
0.00 turns off to Káto Sangrí). The bus stops at a **bus shelter** (left) opposite the road to Káto Sangrí. You follow the disappearing bus for 200m along the road, leaving it at a right bend and turning on to a country lane straight ahead in direction of Mt. Zás. There is a power line on the left.
On the way down, you see the first inhabited pýrgos (Paléologos 1) against the backdrop of Apáno Kástro, the main Venetian fortress in the hinterland of the island ⑫. In the valley below lies a large, noble country residence of
0.15 a newer kind. We cross the **dry-bed**, taking the roadway up left in the direction of the chapel on the hill just in front. At the fork we go straight ahead and, before the
!! left-hand bend beside a wall (right), *inconspicuously right*
0.20 on to the old **stone path** (**P1:** N37°02.887'/E25°26.935'), which used to lead from the Tragéa plateau to the harbour 2. From the kalderími we can soon see the beautiful old (but regretfully locked) cruciform-domed church Agios
★ Artémios 3 and another pýrgos (Baséou or Tímios Stavrós ⑨) in the background. After 6 min., beyond some ruins

3

4

on the right, the path becomes lost in the rock and we let
0.30 ourselves be guided by a wall to a **country lane.**
After passing a polygonal shed (right) you come to the main road. Proceeding left below it for 50m, you find a
0.35 **country lane** on the left, later a footpath which runs be-
0.40 low the road to **Ephraim chapel.** Here you cross the road and enter a track beside a factory (right). After about 200m two mule tracks branch off to the left. We take the second **path**, which leads straight on between walls (**P2:** N37°03.837'/E25°28.581'). Shortly afterwards the rather overgrown path runs left and through a gate.

Walls lead us safely through large olive groves to a lane. We turn left here and again at the next fork. After a dip we
0.50 pass the small village of **Damalás** in the dip to the left, protected by an attractive domed church. We stroll right on the same level through old olive groves to the village
1.05 of **Damariónas.** At the very entrance to the village, at the corner of a house, we head right into a maze of alleys, passing the church and tavern (right), turning right be-
1.10 fore an archway and then down to the overgrown **war memorial** on the asphalt road (**P3:** N37°03.055'/E25° 27.773'). There we have the choice:

To Chalkí: If you want to use mule tracks, descend *15 steps* to the left of the memorial (not of the statue!), go right at the fork which follows immediately and later left in front of a garden gate. Go to the right behind the small bridge and then turn left again directly afterwards, passing the sports field on your right and going through the narrow pass. Then, keeping left of the houses, you'll arrive at the washing facilities in
1.25 **Chalkí.** The village has two tower-houses, one of them being the three-storey Gratsi pýrgos just left of the church 4. Bus departure about 4.35 pm.

1.10 **The way to Filóti** leads up to the right of the monument and further up to the left. At the upper end of the Tragéa plain walk on a road with a great view, surrounded by olive trees. No matter how hard you try, you will not lose your way here and thus have all the time in the world to look out for more pýrgi. Three can be seen at once – two in Chalkí and one in Keramío.

Below Filóti we take the bridge over the hollow, then the track right directly after and later wander up to the left, between gardens beneath Mt. Zás, to the inviting street

1.30 cafés of **Filóti.** The patrons know exactly when the next bus will arrive and that there is still time for refreshments under the plane trees. If you're interested, you will also find another pýrgos, that of the Barozzi family, south of the main church in Filóti. Bus departure about 4.30 pm.

Pýrgi – the tower-houses of Náxos

During the Venetian period from 1207 until 1537 Náxos was the centre of power in the Cyclades. The Venetian vassals of the Duke of Náxos (or Paléologos) built block-like tower-houses for themselves here in the interior of the island, the pýrgi (towers, singular: pýrgos). The indigenous peasants were subservient to these vassals. About 30 such towers are preserved, each named after the owner family. Some have been renovated and are inhabited, others were temporarily used as monasteries after 1537.

Originally they had thick outer walls, windowless apart from embrasures, on a rectangular ground plan, inside which were erected two to three storeys, often with a chapel. In this way a few formed a courtyard with gallery. The accessible roof had battlements. The gateways were very low and could not be passed through standing upright. They were positioned above the terrain and could only be reached via removable wooden stairs. From above they were protected with oriels for pouring boiling oil.

Pýrgi can be encountered on tours ① ② ③ ⑩ ⑫ ⑱.

Besides the Venetian tower-houses two fortified, *round* dwellings from the Hellenistic period have partly been preserved, the Chimárrou and Paléopýrgos towers. They are built seamlessly of marble blocks (p. 32).

⓫ Two villages in the olive groves

On this 3-hour round trip you wander through the olive groves between the still unspoilt villages of Damalás and Damariónas, mostly on country lanes, but also on short tracks. In Damariónas it is possible to enjoy the midday tranquillity in front of the village taverna.
Damalás
■ *7 km, difference in altitude 50m, easy*

AWT 0.00 From the **bus stop** at the branch-off **to Damalás** a little road ascends gently towards Mount Zeus in the background. Below the village you turn right and on the right soon see the articles of pottery decoratively hung up to dry.

On account of the clayey soil in the surrounding area the village has a long pottery tradition. The potter Manolis Limpertás can usually be found in the building next to the potter's wheel. He is only too pleased to explain how the traditional **Sfuni carafe** is – rather laboriously – filled.

0.05 Now it is only a few more paces into the very pretty village of **Damalás**, where you absolutely must take a look at the old olive press on the right below the tiny square; five men used to have to operate it arduously. Continuing on down, you pass another private collection of folklore (right).

0.10 At Pigádia washing area (290m) a concrete track starts ascending, which you turn off at the top by dipping to the right. At the following **fork** you wander on horizontally through the olive groves. After two minutes you go left at the fork and after another minute right! At the end of a

0.15 lengthy stretch of ascending **concrete track** (right a trun-

1

2

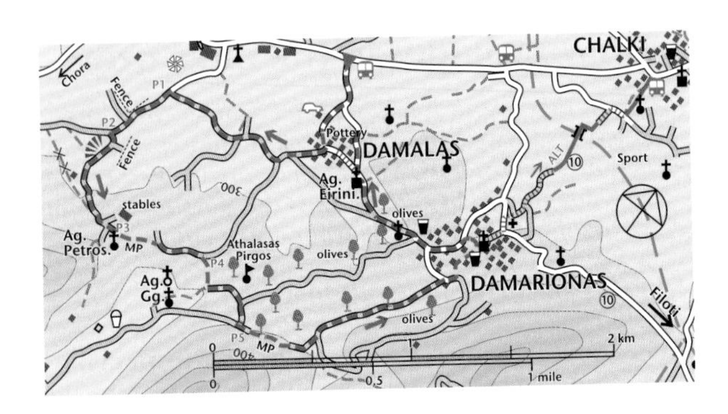

cated windmill) you continue climbing up to the left (**P1:** N37°02.941'/ E25°27.664').

!! 0.20 After the trail dips again, you turn off into the *sharp left branch-off* of an ascending **defile** (on the right an opening in the wall) (**P2:** N37°02.767'/E25°27.592'). After a barrier you turn, 20m before an iron gate, right and enjoy the wide panorama as far as Páros. Further up you skirt an overgrown defile which comes up from the right. On the left, 80m away, are some sheds. Before the hillock the trail

0.30 turns to the right and reaches the plain **Petrus Chapel** (P3: N37°02.552'/E25°27.817', 325m).

Directly above the chapel [1] you find a beaten track which, after 100m, joins a wall-lined mule track [2]. Proceed along this towards the mountain chapel above Filóti. It is not worth making a diversion to the ruins of a St. George's double-chapel down on the right later on.

0.35 Soon you come to a **lane** and, where it ascends in a left bend, turn off right into a broad, shady path (**P4:** N37°02.655'/E25°28.056'). 15m beyond the garden gate

0.40 (right) the path divides. You go left to an ascending **concrete track.** Very skilfully concealed on the left in the groves is the Venetian Athalasas house tower. Go right at the fork (if you do not wish to take the direct route to Damariónas). Further up the roadway divides again after 3 minutes (**P5:** N37°02.568'/E25°28.294', 340m).

Those who go left here soon find a short, but very beautiful monopáti [3]. After it merges into a wide country lane you again have distant views of the island. In a wide left bend you walk round the dip with hundreds of old olive

1.00 trees. At the fork take the easier way down to a **little concrete road.** Here you continue right on the same level and, in **Damariónas**, left down the steps. Then down

3

4

right in front of a masonry bench (1983) and immediately afterwards left through the arch. Further down, beside the church, you then reach the **Platía Potirόu** 4. With taverna and shop – everyday Greece. From there you cross the forecourt of the church and go down four steps.

1.05

Alternative: By going right down the alley, it is possible to stroll along the road leading away from the monument to **Chalkí**, see p. 52. There too one can find an attractive selection of pottery goods.

Those who ramble up left, then turn off right and keep straight on at the power pole find an elegant way out of the village. On the road you go left into a wide valley, at the **fork** down right and then right again through the olive groves. The road going uphill leads to the **Eirini Church** above **Damalás.** From there it is 10 minutes on the road to the main road, where hopefully the bus will soon be zooming down.

1.10
1.15
1.20

To reach your hire car, turn off left into the village after the Eirini Church.

⓬ Apáno Kástro, the Venetian fortress

Mainly following mule tracks, we wander across the extremely verdant valley of Potamiá in 4 to 5 hours. The very beautiful tour then leads on below the Venetian fortress to Chalkí. Water abounds everywhere and Áno Potamiá has a pleasant garden taverna to offer as well.

Road above Ag. Mámas.

Back to there by bus from Chalkí.

■ 10 km, difference in altitude 270m, moderate

AWT In the bus to Chalkí tell the driver you wish to alight at *Ágios Mámas*. (Three minutes beyond Galanádo stands a filling station on the left. Some 400m farther on the road leads over a pass from where you can see a valley and numerous peaks to the left. This is our stop!)
From here you can survey the route of the hike: the three parts of Potamiá can be seen in the green fold down on the left and, on the steep cliffs to the right above, our destination – Apáno Kástro [1].

0.00 In the **saddle** a broad path runs into the valley (straight on at the fork). Soon you behold a barrel-vaulted chapel on the right and later the old church of Agios Mámas [2]. At the very bottom take a few steps to the right along the path running crosswise.

0.11 The official tour "6" leads right at the **portal** (**P1:** N37°03.752'/E25°25.541') and round the grounds in an arc. But it is also possible to open the mesh grid at the portal and continue down to the empty barrel-vaulted chapel without a trail. Turn right along the roadway below.

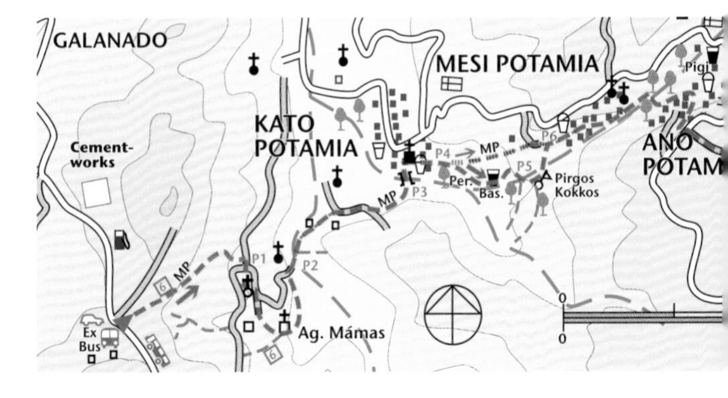

After a few metres you come to the ruins of the seat of the archbishop built in 1707 and, farther down, to the locked, picturesque ruins of the cruciform-domed basilica
0.15 *of* ***Ágios Mámas.*** *Built in the 9th century, it was the main church on the island as well as being, during Venetian rule, the seat of the Catholic archbishop.*

From the portal we follow the trail to wheel ruts into the
0.25 bottom of the valley. In the **ditch** (**P2:** N37°03.770′/E25° 25.729′) we go up right and continue along a splendid path through olive groves. This rich agricultural land is dotted with cypress trees. We proceed straight on at a
0.40 fork, through a hollow and up to **Káto Potamiá.** Leaving the church (with a water tap and adjacent garden inn) to our left, we bear right into the alley and carry on up through the village, about 200m beyond which is a fork (above a manhole cover).

Alternative: To the left is a marvellous panorama path, with views across the valley and its olive trees, leading directly up to Mési Potamiá ③.

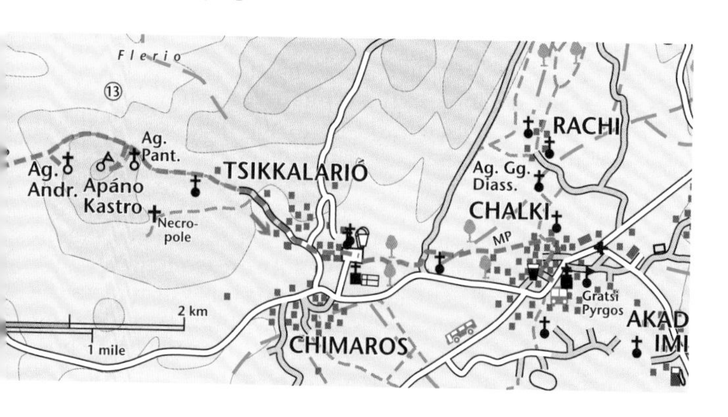

Following the signs downhill, walk past the turn-off to the closed Perivóli garden. After the new garden inn *Basiliko* (right) climb up the street and turn right on top. The
0.45 next turn-off takes you to the right above the **stream** (**P5:** N37°03.963′/E25°26.416′, 100m), which you follow until
0.50 you come to the romantic ruins of the locked **Kokkos Pýrgos** 3 on the right of the path. The embrasures on the top floor date back to less peaceful times.
0.55 Steps lead us up to **Mési Potamiá.** At the well (**P6:** N37°04.067′/E25°26.581′) we start climbing past another
1.00 well and up along a paved path to the left to a **chapel** behind a tree (left). From here we head right down and then, at an old chapel with an imbricated barrel-vaulted roof (right), down left before following a stream for a bit. At a fountain, a wide stepped alley leads up to the right.
!! After 80m we *turn left horizontally* to the main alley through the upper part of **Áno Potamiá.** Here we need to watch out: in the now broader alley are seating steps on
1.05 the left and on the other side a disused **well.** (3 min. straight on you come to the popular garden taverna "Pigí".)
!! *On the right of the well* we go up the steps of the Odos
1.10 Nikolaoy Orfanoy to the **asphalt road.** Just opposite, a roadway runs straight on up in the direction of Apáno Kástro. After 7 min. at a left bend (**P7:** N37°04.013′/ E25°27.209′) the practised Cycladic eye spots a kalderími on the right which, to the left of a wall, leads up into the pass on the left-hand side of the fortress-topped moun-
1.25 tain. Passing the partly painted **Andreas chapel** (right), you wander straight ahead alongside the wall as far as the
1.30 **Panteleimon chapel.** From the opening in the wall in front of this you scramble up the slope to the horseshoe-shaped gun turret, which formerly protected the entrance

to the lower bailey, without a path ④. Phew!!

1.45 ***Apáno Kástro****, the former principal Venetian fortress used to be called Castel d'Alto – the upper fortress – in contrast to the fortress in Chóra, with which there was visual contact. Remains of the main castle building measuring about 50 x 120m may be found on the plateau.*

The rock had been inhabited since prehistoric times, as proven by ancient wall remains and burial sites. In the 13th century it was fortified anew by the Venetians (see p. 45).

2.00 Following the descent we again come to the **Panteleimon chapel** in the saddle. We now stroll right across terraced fields with distant views of Mount Zeus and the Tragéa plateau stretched out in front. Further down, walking between huge rocks, we come to the village of **Tsikkalarió.** Stay on the main alley, turning left at the

2.20 bottom after the washing area beside the **chapel** at the car park.

A shady footpath beneath oaks and mistletoe brings us to a roadway. If you do not care to use the road on the right to Chalkí, go 40 paces up the roadway to the left and then right on to a marked path. First traversing a dry-bed, and

2.40 then olive groves, this likewise leads to **Chalkí** (260m). Keeping to the right, you will find some tavernas to relax in while waiting for the bus.

⑬ Two old youths

The idyllic 4 to 5-hour hike leading to two marble statues mostly does without clearly defined trails, but it is easy to find the way. Long trousers are advisable.
You only have 4½ hours between the arrival of the bus in Chalkí and the return journey from the Koúros, so be sure to enquire about bus times, also for Melanés.
Tsikkalarió, back from AWT 1.35 from the car park at the Koúros. On trail "6" to Ano Potamia and with ⑨ to Tsikkalarió. Total duration about 5½ hours.
■ 11 km, difference in altitude 250m, moderate

AWT 0.00 From the bus stop in **Chalkí** (260m), turn down the alley beside the chemist's shop and go past Giannis' attractive inn. Sorry, no time today!

Head right on the road below, leaving the village, and proceed 300m along the small road between old olive groves, past a chapel (right) as far as a **bridge** with a little house [1] (0.06). There you follow the dirt track to the right and, after 20m, the path left up a simply idyllic path to the village **Tsikkalarió.** The way through the village is fairly flat. At the **end of the village** (0.18), in the midst of a moon landscape, you see the ruins of the mountain fortress Apáno Kástro Further up the valley a **signpost** points left. (0.20)

> **Detour:** *Here a well-beaten track leads in eight minutes to a burial site from the Geometric era (750 BC). A standing stone, similar to a menhir, can be seen* [2] **(P1:** N37°03.832'/E25°27.875', 340m). *About 30 round or elliptic tombs measuring up to twelve metres in diameter have been excavated. The burial gifts from these dolmens are on display in the archaeological museum in Chóra: ceramics, gold jewellery and charred figs and nuts.*

1

2

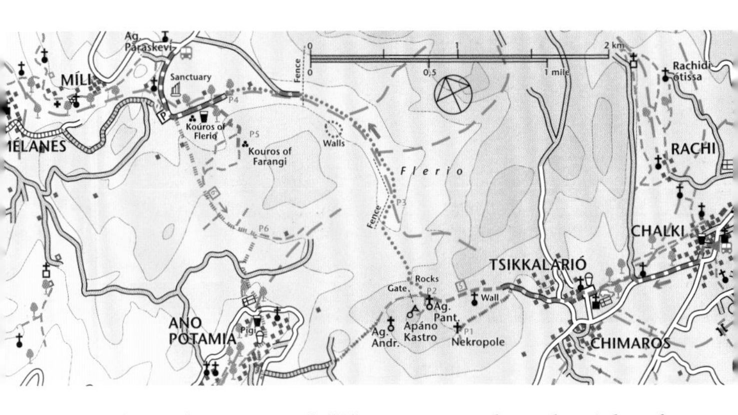

Back on the main trail "5", you proceed on the right of
0.30 a long wall up to **Panteleimon chapel** in the saddle. (Behind it is the ascent to the Apáno Kástro fortress, see p. 59).

Our tour continues 150m beyond the chapel – a good 80m before a gate – to the right of the path at a tall boulder (**P2:** N37°04.100′/E25°27.661′, 335m) without a path across rock slabs ③ and down left before the rocky hill. After the hill you turn right and wind your way without a path through rocky terrain along the left-hand side of the slope down on to the Flério plateau, green in spring,
★ which emanates something mystical. Cairns help to find the well-beaten tracks. Where a fence blocks your progress, cross a sandy dry-bed (**P3:** N37°04.598′/E25° 27.770′). The fence is now on the left. At the end of the valley go past a walled field with wind-bent trees on your left. Open the transverse fence on the left and use the ve-
1.00 hicle tracks on the right of the **dry-bed.** You follow these until they lead up to the right. From there on it is quite strenuous walking at the beginning directly in the rocky
1.15 dry-bed between oleander bushes to a **concrete track**. (**P4:** N37°05.024′/E25°27.212′). Entrance on the right.

After 150m, at a low concrete stele on the left, go left along the newly laid path for six minutes up through the
1.25 ancient marble quarry to the **Koúros of Farangi**, whose legs broke during transport ④ – old photo (**P5:** N37° 04.872′/E25°27.232′). Latterly some experts tend to the view that it could be a virgin. Some details could support that view. Scattered all over the recently laid-out park are further half-carved columns and architectural objects.

Back in the dry-bed, continue down the concrete track

underneath the trees until signs point left. Here lies the
1.35 **Koúros of Flério,** (p. 29, ④).

Koúros statues represent gods or heroes. This prostrate statue must date from the 6th century BC. Due to a flaw in the material they were never finished and have remained in this ancient quarry ever since.

You can buy drinks and small snacks and make yourself feel at home in the lovingly tended paradise-garden.

Thus refreshed, you go left along the already familiar concrete track and down to the car park.

Round trip: To the left of the car park trail "6" leads to *Tsikkalarió,* should you have left your car there. Turn off right at (**P6:** N37°04.512'/ E25°27,049')! The round trip has a total AWT of 3.00.

Up on the right is a new archaeological park, a round-shaped area with a diameter of 40m. This was the shrine to a goddess of fertility and her two strong sons, the pa-
1.40 tron saint of stonemasons. The **bus** stops at around 2.45 pm 800m further up on the main road.

Those who prefer to catch the bus in Melanés proceed through the car park below, up behind the dry-bed and after 100m right. Soon the village can be seen hanging
2.00 above a terraced valley. Go up the alleys from the **lower part** of **Mélanes.** Everywhere giant cocks' heads advertise
2.05 the village's popular chicken inns. The **bus** departs at around 2.35 pm in front of the last of them, Agkyra.

⑭ Drosianí, Lady of the Morning Dew

This breathtakingly stunning round trip leads out of the Tragéa plain along marvellous mule tracks, past the Drosianí church of art-historical importance, up to the mountain village Moní in 4 to 5 hours. Moní and Chalkí offer good places to stop for refreshments.

Chalkí

■ *9 km, difference in altitude 185m, moderate*

AWT In **Chalkí** (260m) the bus stops in front of the large Panagía Protothrónou church, famous for its paintings from seven centuries. As it is mostly closed, head down 0.00 the **alley** beside the chemist's shop and then the second !! *to the right* at the Citron distillery.

★ If you walk on ten metres, you run the risk of having to defer your plans: the small platía with the taverna "Giannis" is a picture-book Greek square. Better keep it in mind for the return leg.

The alley right (see above) marked "4" leads us through the gardens on the edge of the village. We cross a little road slightly to the left and proceed straight on, bearing 0.05 left (sign "Ag. Diassoritis") and come to the **Marína Chapel** (right) above a cistern. Go down left and then right. (Later, to the left is a slight, but most worthwhile detour to the resplendent Byzantine *Diassorítis Chapel.* It has been completely painted and restored inside with frescoes from the 11th century. Accessible in July and August on weekdays from 11.00 am until 1.00 pm.)

Taking a concrete lane which traverses the dry-bed, you 0.10 walk past the chapel (right) in the hamlet **Ráchi** to the far end of the settlement, where you go right and later disregard a whitewashed double chapel on the left. Go right at

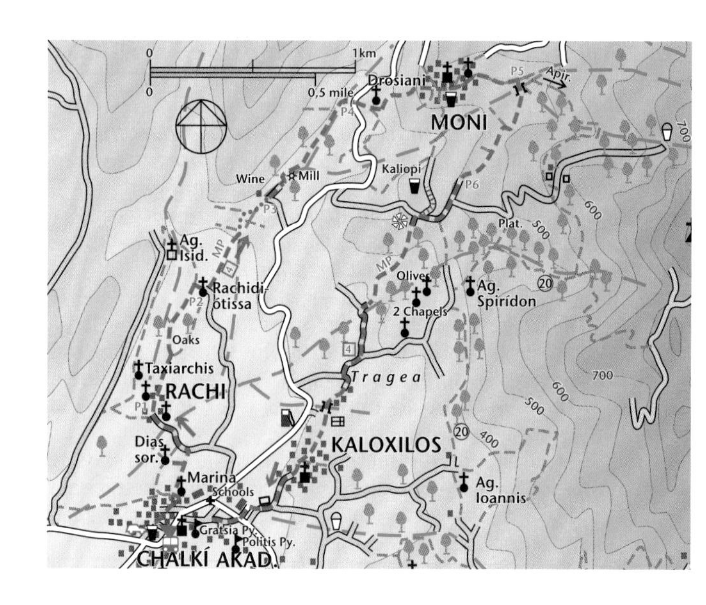

the ruin at the exit from the hamlet. You now proceed

★ along one of the most beautiful Cycladic trails [1], keeping parallel with the counterslope. Our half-way point, Moní, is visible above right in the hills. At the fork you turn down left to the oak wood, at the next one up right on a paved trail. To your left, on the counterslope, the ruins of the Isidorios church with three naves comes into view. When you have almost drawn level with the church,

!! climb up a steep, *naturally stepped path* on the right to the

0.20 superbly situated, but closed **Rachidiótissa Church** [2] (**P2:** N37°04.395'/E25°29.069'). It contains frescoes from the 14th century.

Now continue across the hill, then downhill and left after 20 m. A slightly overgrown monopáti leads gently downhill through large olive groves into a dry-bed and on above the left side of the stream. Shortly afterwards you change sides and the stream is now on your left. Press on through the "stream" between oleander bushes and man-size dragon arum, which lures insects with the odour of rotten meat (p. 14). Further ahead are paths leading uphill both on the right and on the left. 50m beyond a fence traversing the entire streambed (can be opened to the left) you take the shady defile (**P3:** N37°04.586'/E25°29.188')

!! ascending *diagonally to the right* on to a broad **concrete**
0.30 **lane**, where you proceed left/straight ahead. On the left are cisterns in a fenced-off vineyard. 100m beyond the end of the fence we stalk into a transverse dry-bed (to the right a watermill). Along a wall-lined path in the streambed you then come to two paled gates (left). There on the right a splendid monopáti leads up the hill. Skip across the road at the top (**P4:** N37°04.871'/E25°29.582') on to a wonderful, wide paved track and immediately left to the clock-tower in the olive grove!

0.45 *The **Panagía Drosianí,** "Our Lady of the Morning Dew", is, despite its name, the oldest church on the island. The chancel with the three apses from the 4th century BC is the oldest part. In the 7th century three cavernous oratories were added next to it, then in the 12th century both sections were connected with one another by the large rectangular main room.*

The frescoes are famous; in the main cupola the oldest layers are as much as 1400 years old and thus the oldest in the Balkans. This church is open, on 8th September is church dedication day!

From there you stroll on along the kalderími up to the
0.50 **perimeter of Moní.** If you do not intend to stop at the nice panoramic inn "Panorama" (445m, near the church), amble on up through the gently rising village, which otherwise has little to recommend it. At the far
0.55 end, go down between **two chapels** 3 to the old washing troughs just beyond the village, from where a small concrete path leads up to terraced gardens. At a fork drop down to the right and, after a hollow, climb up again. On the way up you come to a small trapezoidal **concrete**
1.05 **bridge** (**P5:** N37°04.945'/E25°30.193'), where the stairway to Apíranthos begins.

3

4

!! But *before that* we go down the marble steps on the right and, after another bridge, up right. On the level of Moní we wander on in horizontal bends. After dropping slightly, we turn off left at the T-fork (sign "8") and continue on the same level – ignoring a right turn-off.

1.20 Reaching a new **country lane** (**P6:** N37°04.702'/E25° 29.938', 390m), which we later stroll down to the right past two monopátia branching off left. The lane is joined by another one on the right (taking it to the right would, after 2 min., afford us a nice spot to rest at "Kaliopi" beneath oak trees!). 70m beyond this junction a two-metre !! wide roadway *forks left* in a right-hand bend. It soon be- 1.25 comes a wall-lined **monopáti.**

Over on the hill to the right are two windmill torsos. We head downhill between some rocks, ahead of us the Tragéa plain with its villages and, towering above them, the three Venetian fortress-house towers and the dome of the church of Kalóxylos. Up here are ***resting places with a view over Mount Zás.

There is no getting lost on the way down. The dome of the church in Kalóxylos is our goal. Two rural chapels lie picturesquely among the olive trees on the left [4]. Below, 1.35 shortly before the **dry-bed** (rocky ledges), begins a roadway through the olive groves. Continue straight ahead at a left turn-off. Along the wayside are a few deserted houses and washing troughs (left), a bridge and a graveyard.

1.50 Alongside the Triáda church of **Kalóxylos** we march 2.00 down to the road, and are guided slightly left to **Chalkí** by the Venetian Gratsía tower-house.

If you are unlucky, you may end up at the Politís tower in Akádimi, a neighbouring village. In which case you will need a few minutes more. Perhaps there is still time for a glass at "Giannis" (**P7:** N37°03.749'/E25°28.936').

⑮ Two churches in the olive grove

The description offers two options, each lasting 2 hours:
A) Ascent from Chalkí to Filóti
B) A circular hike round Chalkí.
Following picturesque paths and country lanes, you pass two important Byzantine churches and three Venetian tower-houses and stroll through numerous olive groves. For somewhere to take a break you have to wait until you get back, half way along spring water is available free of charge.
🚌 Chalkí, A) Back by bus to Chalkí.
■ A) 4 km, altitude difference 140m, easy to moderate
■ B) 5 km, difference in altitude 90m, easy

AWT 0.00 — From the bus stop in **Chalkí** (260m) you follow the markings immediately to the right of the raised church forecourt into a narrow alley. Having crossed a tiny bridge,
!! — you turn off *left before the steps,* now accompanied by a wall on the right. A sunken path runs alongside an olive
0.06 — grove (right), later dropping, and joins a **roadway,** which you take to the left. At two branches to the left you walk straight ahead on gravel until you see, raised up on the left, the old Byzantine church with its cross-vaulted dome
0.10 — **Agíi Apóstoli Metochíou** 1.

The façade of the only two-storey church (10th–11th century) is adorned with exceptionally sophisticated blind arches. An outside staircase leads to the upper chapel. The dome of the painted, unusually tall church rests on four piers. Few remains of wall paintings from the 12th and 13th centuries are preserved. Sometimes open on weekdays from 10.00 am to 2.30 pm.

Continue in the same direction in a left arc through the

1

2

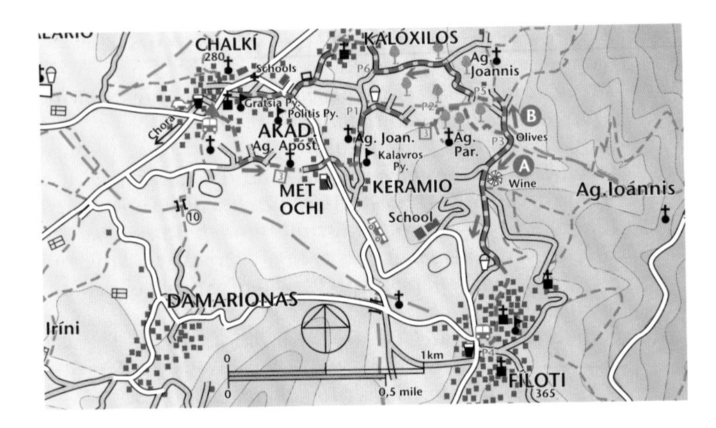

hamlet **Metóchi** to the main road. On the far side of the road lies **Keramío**, where you diagonally climb up past a church (left) to the right. After 80m you turn left at two water meters (right) up to the medieval Venetian tower-

0.15 house **Pýrgos Kalavrós** (right, private). Saunter down the paved alley between the houses.

At the end of the village, on the left, stands the important Byzantine church ***Ágios Ioánnis Pródromos*** *(11th–13th century). It contains the remains of superb frescoes. Three angels surround the pantokrátor, the universal ruler in the cupola. With a little diplomatic skill you can obtain the key in the neighbouring house.*

0.20 If you do not use the **spring** in the hollow further down (**P1:** N37°03.739'/E25°29.473'), turn off up to the right already 40m earlier and gradually walk uphill along a concrete track, later under trees near the stream. You pass two left turn-offs before the old paving stones reappear and

0.25 the path **forks.** (To the right is the Paraskeví chapel.)

3

4

We go left [2] and later ignore the inviting natural steps to
0.30 the right and drop down to the **dry-bed** (**P2:** N37° 03.772'/E25°29.795', 330 m). We climb up the dry-bed for one minute, past a concrete track (left) as far as a path which takes us on up to the right. At a garden gate we again drop to the left and back into the dry-bed (**P3:** N37°03.705'/E25°29.985'). After a few metres a left turn
0.40 takes us up to a **roadway.**

Here **Tour B** goes left (see below).

Ramble up the roadway to the right and, after 200m, over the dry-bed to the right. On the left vines grow on the now concreted path. Below a windmill (left) you cross a
0.45 **small hill** (400m) and see Filóti spread out before you and above it the majestic Zeus. At the fork you naturally take the easier option, in other words the one leading downhill. (Up left, after 250m, a somewhat overgrown monopatí on the right would likewise take us in our direction.)
Where the road joins a larger street at a well, you walk steeply up to the left and over the hilltop at the edge of the village. Then straight ahead and, at the church (left),
1.00 down right to the street cafés of **Filóti** as fast as your legs can carry you! Hungry hikers can expect a satisfying portion in Nicolas' taverna, across the street not much more than coffee [3] (**P4:** N37°03.117'/E25°29.870', 355 m).
Hire car drivers take a taxi or bus back to Chalkí.

Round tour B:
0.40 On the **roadway** you walk left, likewise at the second fork, and turn, 30m before a house, left down a defile [4].
0.45 At the end you come to a **roadway** (**P5:** N37°03.804'/ E25°29.828', 350m), go right and, at the junction, left down a concrete road. At the T-junction at the very end (**P6:** N37°03.856'/E25°29.493', 335m) you stroll right
0.55 and, shortly before **Kalóxilos**, left. Trail "4" then leads
1.00 you past two tower-houses to **Chalkí.**

⑯ Zás

The highest mountain in the Cyclades be... of the supreme Greek deity, Zás – Zeus. For N... popular, 3 to 4-hour tour you should choose a fine ... unless you want to grope through clouds ②. The paths are however well marked and easy to find. Reliable springs are non-existent.

Agía Marína Chapel

■ ***6 km, difference in altitude 390m, moderate-difficult***

To begin the tour in **Filóti**, follow the description on page 77.

AWT 0.00 The bus stops above Filóti at the **branch-off** to **Agía Marína/Zás.** Ascend the road branching up to the right. After the second bend is a short-cut. At the top a level 0.10 stretch of road leads to the **Agía Marína Chapel** (600m). To the right of the chapel a beautiful path runs uphill, first past a house (left), then through sparse woodland (photo left). Having traversed a hollow, you come to roadway merging from the right. About 120m beyond it is a stone bench on the right. Immediately to the right of this lies a sloping **slab of rock** into which is inscribed the Old Greek sentence *Mountain of Zeus, protector of the herds* ①. Its age is uncertain.

Two minutes later, on the right-hand side of the path, 0.25 stands a trough at the **Levgassa spring.** At the fork which follows immediately one climbs up to the right; the high vegetation is now behind you. Two limekilns (**P7:** N37°02.294'/E25°30.777', 745m) lie along the way, which 0.30 then leads towards a **high wall.** There you head up right, through prickly spurge bushes ②. The wall is joined by a fence, but you leave this already after 30m by going up

1

2

right. Having scaled a **foothill**, the trail becomes flatter and, clearly marked, leads up the **summit of Zás (P6:** N37°01.818'/E25°30.138'). Together with other hikers you enjoy the all-round view of the Cyclades. Humidity often obscures the view in summer, so Samos' Mount Kérkis (1.440m) is not visible, as it might be in winter. At least, that's what some locals profess ...
The way back to the Marína Chapel or further down to Filóti is described in walk 17.

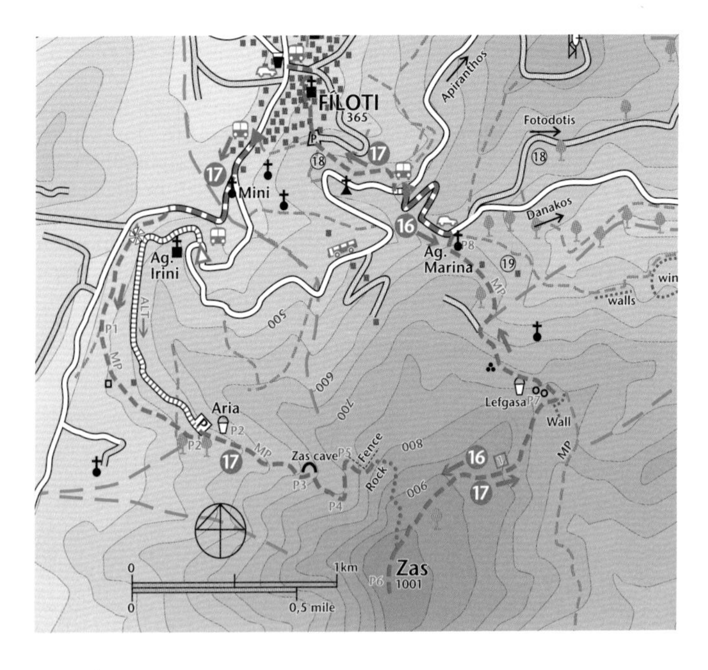

⑰ The cave of Zeus

Today we're going slightly alpine – by tackling the western side of Zeus, the highest mountain in the Cyclades! Besides protection against the sun and wind, and a bottle of water, a torch may also come in very handy for the Zeus cave. Although a head for heights is not required for the 4 to 5-hour mountain tour, orientation skills are important, for we follow not just old paved tracks but cross-country trails too.

Filóti, maybe bus Ag. Marína – Filóti

■ *8 km, difference in altitude 650m, difficult*

▷ *Map see left*

Shortcut of ½ hr.: Ask for the bus to stop about 600m beyond Filóti at the right branch-off to "Aría Spring" and gradually walk up the little road to the right of Irini church as far as the car park at the Aría spring (**P2**).

AWT

0.00 True friends of mule tracks on the other hand alight already at the *second bus stop* in **Filóti** (345m) and gaily set off up the main street in the direction of Apíranthos. About 300m after the stop take the road to the right beside the

0.03 **mini-chapel**, towards Chimárrou. You follow this road 60m before a right branch-off to an industrial building. There you veer diagonally up to the left on rocky slabs

0.15 and on to a **path.** It later becomes more visible, then almost at once skirts a windmill (left) and is transformed into a wonderful mule track which leads left uphill. For 10 min. it has no shade: Wedding fireworks set fire to the trees in the summer of 2006.

0.25 At the **fork** (**P1:** N37°04.083'/E25°26.588') in front of a walled field you wander left up through the gate. After

0.30 going through further gates you see **house ruins** below

on the right. From there you proceed, later in a left arc past houses (left), until you see the steep Mount Zeus [1]. Above retaining walls is the car park and beyond that a 0.40 shady place to rest with the **Aría well** (**P2:** N37°02.204'/ E25°29.625', 510m). Your bottle of water replenished, the climb can now commence.

A recently laid paved path forms the first part, later a steep track leads up through the rocks, past another well, 0.55 to the roughly 100 m deep **Cave of Zeus** [2]. (**P3:** N37° 02.076'/E25°29.987', 630m.) Here he is said to have spent his first years as a god, but this is claimed of quite a number of caves (p. 76). Without a torch that must have been an inhospitable childhood. Inside the cave, to the right, are quite sizeable rooms which one tends to overlook at first.

In the gorge one gazes up at the precipitous mountain in disbelief [3]. But, no fear, up there on the left we will be hiking on perfectly safe tracks. The stony path first leads on up through the gorge and then turns left out of the gorge 1.05 *below a **field of scree*** (**P4:** N37°02.023'/E25°30.057', 1.10 600m) and runs rather steeply uphill as far as a **fence,** parallel with a wall (**P3:** N37°02.118'/E25°30.076', 740m). The magnificent view compensates for the beads of sweat. Follow the fence up to the right. Where the fence turns to the left near some rocks (right), follow it. Where the rocks finish, the path disperses and you have to find your way up in zigzags. On the left you catch a glimpse of the mountain village of Apíranthos nestling in the dip. Having reached the flatter stretch, use the well-trodden paths on the right to climb up to the peak (**P6:** N37°01.818'/ E25°30.138').

1.35 A simple concrete block marks the **summit of Zás** (also Za or Zefs); we have reached the highest point in the Cyclades, 1001 metres above the harbour of Náxos town and more than 600m above Filóti. The people appear to have great respect for Zeus: here there is neither a chapel nor an antenna to disturb the majesty of the mightiest of the Greek Gods (p. 76). After using the all-round view to refresh our knowledge of island place-names we drink to his health.

To return to Filóti, you take the same path for 300m to the left of a group of trees, then swing right towards the Bay of Apóllonas and follow the gently descending path "2". A more frequented trail, it runs downhill on red earth to the right of the top of a foothill, then drops more steeply. Spread out in the sea on the right are the Small Cyclades, sheltered at a distance by the long island of Amorgós.

2.10 At the end of an accompanying wall (right) you swing left in the direction of Filóti and come to round **lime kilns** (**P7:** N37°02.294'/E25°30.777', 745m), later still past the

2.20 **Legvassa well.** Awaiting you on the left-hand side of the path is a bench. Up on the rock to the right of it you discover an Ancient Greek inscription: Mountain of Zeus, protector of the herds (1 p. 71). The marvellous paved

2.30 path 4 ends at the chapel **Agía Marína** (**P8:** N37°02.545'/ E25°30.493').

2.45 Now turn into the road on the left and elegantly shorten the serpentine bends to get down to the **main road.** The afternoon bus drives past here.

3.05 Go left along the road for about 50m and then, thirsty, descend the stairway, later crossing the car park to the right, to **Filóti,** where those nice landladies are already waiting to receive us. Kyriakí cooks wonderfully in her *Baboulás.*

Zeus and Dionysos, Gods on Náxos

At the beginning of all times, the Terra Mater, Gaia, the goddess of the earth, appeared out of chaos. In her sleep, she bore Uranos out of herself and took him as her husband.

Kronos and his sister Rhea, as well as other *Titans,* resulted from this nowadays no longer conceivable relationship. The two of them also united, upholding the family's tradition, and parented the *goddesses* Hera (later the Roman Juno, protector of the military aristocracy), Hertia (the Roman Vesta, goddess of the domestic hearth) and Demeter (Ceres, goddess of the fields) as well as the *gods Zeus* (Jupiter), Poseidon (Neptune) and Hades (Pluto).

The three men divided up the world among themselves: Zeus took Olympus and thus domination; his brothers had the sea and the underworld. **Zeus,** the highest of the gods, lord of heaven and earth, the philanderer of the pantheon, is said to have spent his youth in a cave on Náxos ⑰, brought up by an eagle. He also took his sister Demeter as his wife, who bore the gods Ares (Mars, the Roman god of war), Eilythia, Hebe and Hephaistos (Vulcan). From Zeus's relationships with 15 other godly sisters, there resulted, among others, Artemis, Apollo, Hermes and Aphrodite. Artemis (Roman Diana) is the goddess of the hunt; Apollo represents law and order and peace; Hermes (Roman Mercury) is the *protector of wanderers,* shepherds, tradesmen and rogues, while Aphrodite (Venus) is the goddess of sensual love and beauty.

Zeus did not just have his way in heaven. Meanwhile, there were lovely princesses on earth, too. Without conceit he approached them in various forms, for example as a bull, swan and even as the husband of one of the women he desired. Thus the *Heroes* Minos, Perseus, Helena and Herakles, in addition to fifteen others, were born. They were, however, only half-gods, representing the link between heaven and earth.

Semele, the mortal king's daughter from Thebes, bore him the god **Dionysos** (Roman Bacchus), according to legend in the Jénnesis cave (birthplace) near Engáres on Náxos ②. He was the god of wine and fertility. Dionysos gave Náxos the wine, at that time considered the best in Greece. In his second capacity he took care of Ariadne, who had been left behind by Theseus on the beach on Náxos when he returned after killing the Minotaur in Crete. Through the partner exchange Ariadne rose to become a (demi-)goddess, while the unfaithful Theseus plunged his father Aigéus into disaster, i.e. the sea. The name *Aegean* is just about the only tangible fact to have remained from the era of the gods.

⑱ The mysterious monastery

The glorious, 3½ to 4-hour hike begins in Filóti, leads to a deserted monastery and then along mule tracks through rolling countryside to the pretty mountain village of Apíranthos. The bus returns at about 4.15 pm. One hour could be saved by not getting out of the bus until the branch-off "Agía Marína/Zas"!
Filóti or Ag. Marína with bus back to car
■ *9 km, difference in altitude 270m, moderate*

AWT 0.00 From **Filóti bus station** at the cafés continue 30m up the ascending road before turning off left. On the level concrete track left of the chemist's it is 50m to a bakery (right), where numerous steps begin, marked "2". Higher up, after passing under a low arch, climb the steps on the left, then those on the right in front of the *church*. Shortly 0.05 after take the steps on the left. **Narrow steps** lead you left, then right. At the fork climb the steeper steps to the 0.10 left. Having finally reached the **car park**, you understand what "sloping village" means (**P1:** N37°02.925'/E25°29.928', 435m).

On the left we are tempted to take a wall-lined mule track – that is more to our taste. It climbs straight up 1 0.20 and, after tight bends, comes to the **main road.**

After a 60m climb you reach the bus stop at the branch-off to Danakós (see above) and go up the small road on the right. After the second bend you discover the path on 0.30 the right, which offers a shortcut to the **Agía Marína** chapel (**P2:** N37°02.545'/E25°30.493', 600m).

At the chapel we turn off the road to the left and take the level dirt track straight ahead. With a spring in our step we wander along above terraces, gardens and groves, be-

1

2

neath oak and olive trees, until we imagine we see a Venetian fortress-house tower [2]. But it is supposed to be a fortress-like **monastery** (**P3:** N37°03.032′/E25°31.270′, 480m). — 0.50

The enchantingly situated Moní Christóu Fotodótis (light-bringing Christ) turns out to be a 12–13m high rampart. Inside a church has been integrated half way up. The iconostasis and floor show iconoclastic representations of animals. Above this, apart from a few monks' cells, the curtain wall is hollow.

It is assumed that the early Christian church from the 6th century was heightened with lateral ramparts in the 16th century and expanded into a monastery with internal stairway. This existed until 1903.

Accessible June to September, church dedication day 5th August.

After a short stretch back on our previous path, we turn right (to the north) and continue horizontally above a private dwelling with vineyard on the quiet track "3" leading to the opposite slope. Going straight ahead/right in the gap, we then follow the beautiful track along the slope to the right up to the **saddle.** There is a gate here and another *directly behind,* barely visible in a fence (**P4:** N37°03.251′/E25°31.255′, 660m). Then we see Apíranthos on the other side of the valley. — 1.00 !!

★ Strolling along a monopáti above a plateau (right) [3], it is a pleasure to proceed to a second **saddle** above the wide valley of Apíranthos. The continuation of the track, which has slightly disintegrated here, is in the direction of the previous path, on the right beside a wall (**P5b:** N37°03.427′/E25°31.170′, 585m). At the end of the wall surrounding the oak grove you descend to the left in zigzags to a **T-fork** with fig tree (**P6:** N37°03.535′/ — 1.10, 1.20

E25°31.167′, 560m). From there left downhill, through a ditch and up the other side. Keeping to a stony path, you
1.30 proceed beneath oaks [4] to pumps on the **valley floor** (**P7:** N37°03.602′/E25°30.934′).
On the far side you ascend a sunken path. Reaching a country lane, go right at its concrete fork and then left past a house, returning to the lane further up on the left. In front of a large retaining wall you turn off right and
1.40 come to a path behind the **Eleuferius Chapel.**
Beside the sports ground you come to the road and a little
★ later to a right-hand bend. There steps lead up to the
2.00 beautiful, elongated **platía** in **Apíranthos.** Just before it, on the right, is *Amorginós* with good food and grand views. The bus stop is another five minutes away.

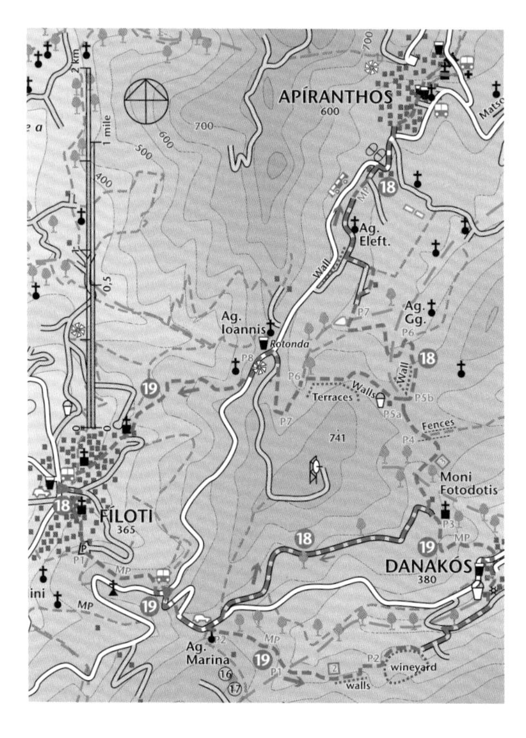

⑲ The source in Danakós

The 5½-hour tour leads down into the valley of Danakós and back up again along old marble steps to the restored monastery Fotodótis. Here the hike could be shortened by one hour. Otherwise it takes you on over two hills and down to Filóti.
Danakós not only has a source to offer, but also places to stop.
Ag. Marína, Round tour.
■ *7 km, diff. in altitude 2 x 200 m, moderate or difficult*
▷ *Map see previous page*

AWT 0.00 Leave the bus beyond Filóti at the **stop** "Agía Marína" (aka "Zás" or "Zefs") and go up the road that branches off. On the right after the second bend you find a well-beaten path that provides a short cut to the right. A level section 0.10 of road later leads to the **Agía Marína** chapel (**P1:** N37° 02.545'/E 25°30.493', 610m)

20m to the left of the chapel you find the shady trail "2" dropping down into the valley [1], on the left side of which lies a heavily overgrown ravine. Having ignored a 0.25 left turn-off, you traverse a **dry-bed** (**P1:** N37°02,551'/ E25°30,724') and now have a better view down into the ravine. About 70m after passing retaining walls (right) and a gate, the path drops about 20m in the fall line (sign "2"). When you re-emerge from the trees, you see on the 0.30 right a **little gate** into a vineyard (**P2:** N37°02.589'/E25° 30.910', 520m).

After small zigzags to the left of it a horizontal stretch be-0.35 gins below the vineyard (right). Later a **roadway** leads in to the valley and to a fairly wide sand road, which you follow to the right. Shortly before the village, at the end of

1

2

the retaining wall on the left, steps lead down left to
0.50 **Danakós source** (410m) [2]. A giant plane shades the idyllic place and one has to repress the desire to lie down in the crystal-clear water! Downstream are the ruins of mills fed by water from upstream. Already before the mills you cross the stream by the bridge and find a café on the right. Steps and alleys bring you up through the village to the little taverna Stefanos above the car park. To the left of it a concrete track ascends, from which concrete steps branch off. Further up you cross the road 20m diagonally to the right to marble steps, which are more pleasing to walk on. A wide paved path, a kalderími overlooking the island of
1.15 Donoússa, leads up to the tower-like **Fotodótis monastery-castle** (**P3:** N37°03.032'/E25°31.270', 480m) [3] (see p.78).

> ***Shortcut:*** If you wish to shorten the hike or return to the car, take the country lane going left at the *fork* in front of the monastery to the **chapel Agía Marína** (Total AWT 1.35). Proceed right there and follow the description on page 75 to **Filóti!**
> (Hire car drivers could however also cover the section between Ioánnis and Marína chapels from AWT 2.20 by bus at around 4.20 pm!)

1.15 The ascending way is marked with "3" from here and, at the fork in front of Fotodótis monastery, runs to the right, on above a holiday house with vineyard (right,), into a
!! transverse stream and behind that *up right* on a very beautiful path alongside a fence (right). As a sunken path it
1.25 leads to **two gates** (**P4:** N37°03.251'/E25°31.255', 660m), which come one after another at a distance of ten metres. Behind the second gate you go to the left and, for quite a while, on the right side of a wall, always enjoying a fabulous view over Apíranthos. Arrows have been sprayed on

the following saddle (**P5a:** N37°03.427'/E25°31.170', 585m). (Along the wall on the right is the way to Apíranthos, see ⑱, from AWT 1.10.)

In front of the left corner of the wall you descend left on the polished slabs and find the rather hidden sunken path

!! *on the left.* It leads to a **source** in a small meadow. From

1.30 here you go up to the right beside the fence until where a

1.45 **mule track** begins. This goes right in the direction of St. John's church with the offset roof ④ and later in a left curve towards terraced fields.

!! Already *before* that the mule track leads down into the tree-covered valley. 30m above the trees the walls briefly widen. After crossing a barrier, you find yourself in the

2.10 **ditch** (**P6:** N37°03.444'/E25°30.787', 575m), where steps lead up left.

2.15 At the top you swing **to the right** (**P7:** N37°03.359'/E25° 30.722'). Here a mule track starts, passing through several

2.20 gates before reaching the **road** and ending at Agios Ioánnis church (620 m) on the steep hillside. The new panorama inn *"Rotonda"* beside it seems truly "aloof". This is where you may wish to stop the bus to Agía Marína or Filóti at around 4.20 pm if that is where your car is parked.

But if you go left 100m slightly down the road, you discover another small chapel down on the right. Proceeding even further along the road, you see – 20m after the place-name sign – a mule track in front of a fence on the right, below the guardrail (**P8:** N37°03.419'/E25°30.569').

Initially it descends alongside the power poles. From the saddle you then get a view of Filóti, which you later reach

2.45 to the right of the **church** on the knoll. You take a few paces to the right above a flat roof, down steps and past the large church (right) to the bus stop on the road in

2.50 **Filóti.** You can unwind again after the strenuous hike in one of the shady cafés. Regrettably the bus already comes at 4.30 pm.

⑳ From Fanári down to Tragéa

After a short ascent up Fanári, the third-highest mountain on Náxos, this very striking 5-hour hike first leads along an old stepped trail, then for ten minutes across a rather arduous rocky streambed down to Tragéa plain. On its upper perimeter you stroll through olive groves and reach your deserved chill-out spot in Chalkí.
🚗 Chalkí and on with bus/taxi to Apíranthos.
■ 9 km, difference in altitude 580m, moderate to difficult

AWT 0.00 From the upper **bus stop in Apíranthos** at the memorial (570m) you enter the "marble village" on the right of the large Church of the Assumption, ascending the steps on the right after 30m. At the top you turn right and, 15m beyond the power pole, take the steps leading left ("1887"). Keeping in the same direction, you turn off left in front of a garden wall and, after 10m, up steps on the right. Without turning off, you head straight on to a T-junction and there left up to the **car park** (**P1:** N37° 04.381'/E25°31.181'). — 0.05

In the same direction you climb steeply and, 20m after the tall **water reservoir**, go left up the rocky path ⬜1. Little walls on the downhill side facilitate the pathfinding. — 0.10

0.20 After tight serpentine bends you reach a gap in the wall.
★ Here begins a wonderful, wall-lined monopáti which leads out of the rocky zone.

Further up you go right where the path forks, come to a **roadway** (**P2:** N37°04.464'/E25°30.784') and march up to the right for three minutes. — 0.30 At a transverse wall on a small saddle you turn up left and arrive at the **summit of Mount Fanári** (883m). — 0.40 Apart from the visually unsuccess-

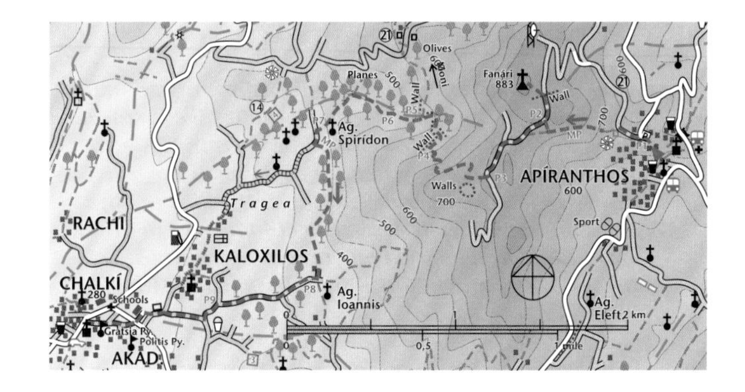

ful chapel there is nothing to impair the distant view. Lying at your feet is the Tragéa plain with Chalkí. To the northwest you can make out the stepped trail for the way down, which from here looks more daunting than it is.

Returning the same way, you are soon back in the wide saddle and walk along the roadway on the next hill until a **left bend.** On the right below there are enclosed pastures [2] (**P3:** N37°04.264'/E25°30.567'). At this point you turn off down to the right, continuing outside the walls. A little further down you turn off right and find a skilfully built stepped trail into the valley [3].

0.50 **saddle**
0.55 **left bend**

You saunter downhill in elegant wide curves. Where the zigzags end, you have to pay more attention to the little red dots again, which lead in front of a transverse **field wall** (**P4:** N 37°04.367'/E 25°30.378').

1.20 **field wall**

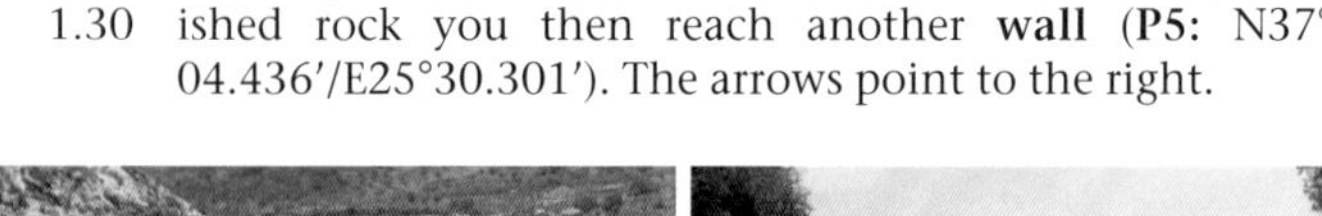

Here you go right, beside the wall and proceed down left in a dry-bed covered with oleander. On smoothly polished rock you then reach another **wall** (**P5:** N37° 04.436'/E25°30.301'). The arrows point to the right.

1.30 **wall**

3

4

!! But not for us, we don't want to go to Moní, *we go left*. We cross the smooth rock to the left side of the stream 10m further down, thus avoiding the cataracts even further down, find a path leading downhill; after two minutes a path leads through a gate back into the dry-bed and pass-

1.35 es an overgrown **cattle trough** (left).

Now stay in or on the left of the stream for about ten strenuous minutes. Cairns indicate the best passages

!! through the large boulders. A *branch-off up left* (**P6:** N37° 04.443'/E25°30.182') avoids the scree in the streambed. But then the going gets easier down beneath plane trees on terraces. At the lower edge of the terraces you descend

1.45 a **mule track** to the left below the picturesquely situated chapel Agios Spiridon ④.

1.50 After a gate you reach a **roadway** (**P7:** N37°04.402'/E25° 29.901', 410m). Go 80m left down this, where a dream path leads on up left. (The roadway would be a shortcut to Kalóxilos.) Two minutes later it becomes horizontal. You now promenade beneath oaks, later in an olive grove, above the abundantly irrigated and fertile plain of Tragéa, which is dotted with over one hundred thousand olive trees.

Our panorama path ends below a holiday house (right) at

2.10 a **country lane** (**P8:** N37°03.939'/E25°29.909'). Opposite, up left, is the St. John's chapel. Although closed, it affords us a wonderful place to rest.

The country lane takes us down to the right, straight on at

2.20 the branch to the left, and further down. At the **fork** (**P9:** N37°03.872'/E25°29.501') shortly before Kalóxilos you head left towards Kerámi for a bit and, at the next branch-

2.25 off, down right into a defile. After a dilapidated **ware-house** (right) you follow wheel ruts in the left-hand bend of the road, go left in front of the school and diagonally right across the main road. Past two Venetian tower-hous-

2.35 es we reach **Chalkí**. Perhaps we still have time for the plá-tia and *Giannis* taverna ...

㉑ Tour around Fanári

The impressive tour takes in both rough and rocky and also bucolic countryside. It lasts 6-7 hours, but towards the end offers a short-cut to Chalkí. (Total 5½ hours.) Paths are used almost throughout, one road section is a slight timesaver. Some experience in pathfinding is useful for the ascent at the end of the full tour.
🚗 Apíranthos and full round tour.
🚗 Chalkí and continue by bus/taxi to Apíranthos.
■ 11 km, difference in altitude 525m, difficult

AWT 0.00 From the *upper* bus stop at the war memorial in **Apíranthos** (570m) it is just 30m along the main alley to the steps which lead us up right. At the top we go right for 15m. At the power pole we proceed left up the steps; written on the railing on the left is "1887". Keeping in this direction, we turn off left in front of a garden wall and, after 10m, up more steps to the right. Without turning off, we continue to a T-junction, where, further up to the left, we 0.05 find a **car park** (**P1:** N37°04.381'/E25°31.181').

In the same direction we take the concrete track up to the 0.10 **water reservoir**. 20m beyond this the trail from Moní comes down – our way back later on. We march straight ahead along the concrete track. Down on the right lies a fertile hollow, out at sea the elongated Amorgós and a few uninhabited islands. Ten meters after the concrete pavement begins we leave the roadway by going right. On the 0.15 right of the now almost level trail stands a small **house.** Glancing behind us, we see the summit chapel of Fanári.

0.25 At the **wall opening** (**P2:** N37°04.987'/E25°31.151') the old monopáti, which was covered by the roadway up to 0.30 here, leads on. It takes us up onto the **saddle** in front of

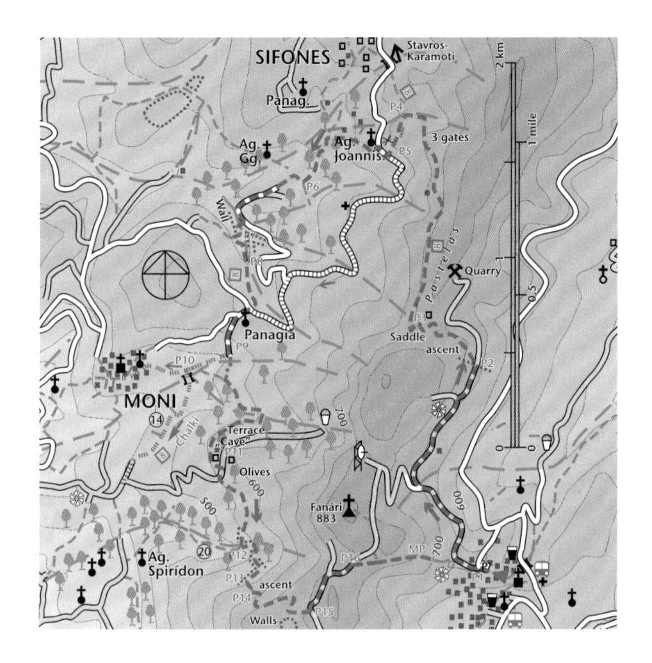

the Pastelás massif (**P3:** N37°05.065′/E25°31.001′, 785m). Now we can see across to Páros and down to Moní.

Tight serpentine bends 1 lead downhill and later, slightly sloped, to the right, in a northerly direction. Above a

0.45 **stone hut** the path continues towards the scattered village of Sífones. Rising up in the background are the notched marble mountains of Kinídaros. A few sections of the path have fallen away and have to be circumvented.

0.55 Passing the last of three **gates**, we bear half-left without a

1.00 path until reaching the **ditch** further down. There we

!! leave the trail "8" *to the left* (**P4:** N37°05.689′/E25°30.938′). A distinct goat track runs, later alongside an overgrown monopáti, towards a chapel. Where the monopáti veers right, the goat track leads us a further 50m through a gate

1.05 to the **road** (**P5:** N37°05.566′/E25°30.834′).

> ***Short-cut:*** The trail described below calls for time and stamina for the climb back up. Staying on the road saves half an hour as far as the Panagía Chapel.

If you choose the old route into the valley, you go up the road for a bit, turn off left and come to the neglected Byzantine **Ioánnis Chapel** 2. From there you descend, continuing in the left-hand bend at the bottom. Then left

at the fork which follows. The wall-lined path shaded by oak trees is still used and well preserved. At another fork (**P6:** N37°05.402'/E25°30.531') you saunter right over a

1.25 hilltop and, after a steeper descent, reach a **country lane.** As a steeply dropping concrete track this finally reaches

1.30 the **valley.**

!! There, below/in front of terraces, you turn *sharp right* and discover a path going left at the water channel. After 30m, at the end of the wall on the right, it runs up right (**P7:**

!! N37°05.354'/E25°30.315', 495m). Then, in the *first right-hand bend, in a small clearing,* you should not overlook

!! the *inconspicuous branch-off* to the left! Trail "8" leads back into the streambed, which you follow for a further *4 min.* Then the path leads to the right and uphill for 8 min.

1.40 (**P8:** N37°05.354'/E25°30.315'). Before you reach the **road** at the top, the path may be covered with grass.

On the far side you cross a "traffic island" and after 50m walk left at the fork in front of the Panagía Chapel. A

1.45 steep concrete track leads down into a dip, where a **defile** branches off right (**P9:** N37°04.976'/E25°30.274').

> ***Short-cuts to Chalkí:*** This defile runs down to a trapezoidal concrete slab, which forms a bridge (**P10:** N37°04.945'/E25°30.193'). Going down the steps straight ahead, thus following ⑭, you come to Chalkí. Total AWT 2.40.
>
> Go right for 8 min. to reach Moní – although there are no buses there, it is also possible to reach Chalkí by taking ⑭ in the opposite direction.

1.45 If you want/have to return to Apíranthos, you come to a gate on the roadway after 3 min. Beyond it you walk about 100 meters without a path until, up at a solitary little oak tree, you traverse the somewhat decrepit path which ascends to the left. Later it swings to the right in the direction of Fanári ③ and becomes a paved kalderími liberally sprinkled with oleander bushes. Right in the

!! middle of these bushes *red dots on the right* draw attention

2.05 to a sandy **branch-off**! A well-beaten track marked with red dots runs up to a terrace and then on alongside trees. It ends at a large stone slab, which has been hollowed into

2.10 a **cave** (**P11:** N37°04.634′/E25°30.198′, 555m).

Above, slightly to the left, runs an overgrown roadway, which you go down as far as a sort of "right-hand bend" ④. Below the bend a mule track leads left directly beside the fence. You have to avoid another collapsed section be-

★ fore it becomes truly romantic (see back cover). The path

2.20 ends in front of the slabs of rock of a **streambed**, where you follow the oleander bushes up to the left (**P12:** N37°04.436′/ E25°30.301′).

At the corner of the wall (right) you follow the beaten track to the right through a left-hand bend as far as the next wall corner. Continue alongside the wall (right) for a further few meters – then red dots (**P13:** N37°04.367′/ E25°30.378′) guide you up left to where the serpentine bends start (**P14:** N37°04.337′/E25°30.382′, 570m). Artfully they lead uphill and end above the rocks in front of a field wall. Here you continue up in the same direction to a

2.55 **roadway** (**P15:** N37°04.264′/E25°30.567′). Go left along this until you catch sight of Apíranthos down below (**P16:** N37°04.416′/E25°30.752′, 800m). The path descending to the right is well marked. Proudly you take another look up at Fanári. That certainly was some achievement today!

3.20 Hopefully you still have a little time to spare for **Apíranthos** – the "marble village".

㉒ A lonely chapel

This very enjoyable 5-hour round-trip on old stone paths and country lanes through woods and gardens shows the variety of landscapes which Náxos has to offer. Although partly shaded, it has only one spring with water. Along the route is an age-old chapel, now closed, which houses important frescoes. However, the bus timetable only allows less than 6 hours for the hike!
🚌 Apíranthos
■ 9 km, difference in altitude 100m, moderate to difficult

AWT 0.00 From the **second bus stop in Apíranthos** at the war memorial (590m) you enter the town across the street, but before the first houses immediately turn down right and under the road bridge. The stone path divides 30m beyond that – we head down the island trail "1" to the right (...and will return, tired and thirsty, along the other path). The wide paved path drops pleasantly [1] and is later shaded by oaks. At a fork you go up to the right. You 0.20 can overlook the right **branch-off** to the three-aisled, but unadorned Johannes-Theologos church (**P1:** N37°04.826'/ 0.25 E25°31.740'; 500m). Disregard a **left branch-off** too. Pro- 0.35 ceed up and down, later alongside a **wooden railing.** Already when descending, you notice, below the wind rotors on the horizon, on the right-hand side of the hill in 0.45 the middle distance the Kyriakí chapel. After the **bridge** in the valley (**P2:** N37°05.186/E25°32.296', 415m) you tramp up the wide kalderími through an olive grove [2]. 1.00 At the farmhouse a detour leads right to the **Kyriakí Chapel.**

It commands spectacular views from its ridge-top perch. Its interior houses a rarity: The wall painting from the

1

2

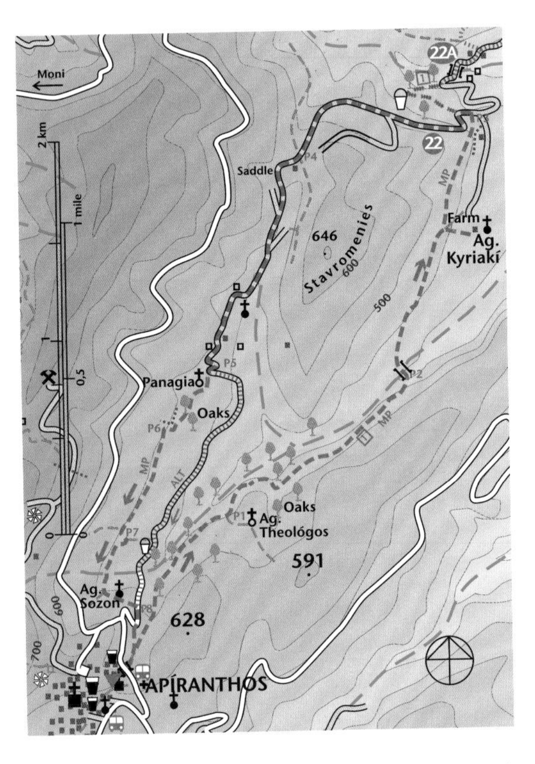

iconoclasm, the iconoclastic controversy in the 8th and 9th centuries. In those days the ideas of Islam also influenced Christianity, including that of prohibiting the pictorial representation of God. During the hundred-year controversy church paintings emerged with geometric and floral motifs (see p.17). That explains why animals (birds and fishes) are depicted here in the apse. Unfortunately the chapel has been closed since the restoration in 2016. However a display board provides a few impressions, as does a tiny peep-hole.

Back on the main route you wander right as far as the

1.15 **brick-steps** which interrupt the old track (**P3:** N37° 05.909'/E25°32.599', 450m).

Alternative: From here tour 22a leads to Moutsoúna (see below). But from there buses only run back to Chóra in July and August.

1.15 To return to Apíranthos, go left along the wide roadway, first round two serpentine bends and then left uphill in a

broad arc. On the opposite slope are the cavernous emery mines (p. 94). A material ropeway runs down to the harbour in Moutsóuna.

1.35 After the **saddle** (**P4:** N37°05.838′/ E25°32.000′) the track becomes narrower and visually more pleasant. Proceeding down a left-hand branch-off into the valley, you come round two **tight bends**, above which, scarcely visible, stand the ruins of a house. Then follow a small farmhouse (left) and finally a **ditch** with more ruins (right).
1.50
1.55

!! After the following knoll you must watch out: *Branching off to the right is a monopáti!* (**P5:** N37°05.220′/E25° 31.688′).

Shortcut: If short of time, stay on the country lane!

The monopáti leads in two minutes to the romantic ruins of the **Panagía Double Chapel** with the remains of wall paintings. The path proceeds left through a grove of oaks [3], accompanied by a retaining wall on the right. Where this ends, you continue along the grass-covered track directly above the left terrace wall. Immediately after a **gate** the path first twists 10m right, then left (**P6:** N37°05.048′/ E25°31.524′, 500m). Some peasants with mules use the horizontal path. Steps lead down to a T-junction. Here you go left and *after 10m right* (**P7:** N37°04.598′/E25° 31.285′). (Down straight ahead is a well beside the country lane.)

2.00
★
2.15
!!

It is a pleasure to stroll between the fields and gardens of the farmers [4] until the path swings left. Passing a chapel (left), you descend a few steps back to the **lane** (**P8:** N37°04.585′/E25°31.371′). There you proceed right, in the lane's right-hand bend straight ahead and on up the path to **Apíranthos!** The best place to relax beneath a plane tree is the taverna *O Plátanos.*

2.30
2.40

㉒A The abandoned mines

This more than 3-hour follow-on treck to tour 22 (from Apíranthos altogether 5 hours) leads down to Moutsoúna harbour, with beach and pleasant inns. Buses only serve Chóra (3.45 pm) in July and August!
The tour runs past abandoned tunnels from the emery mines, the loaded buckets of the material ropeway from 1929 still hovering overhead. A spring may be found along the way, which mostly follows stony paths.
■ 8 km, difference in altitude 450m, moderate

AWT 1.15 From the **brick-steps** (**P3:** N37°05.912′/E25°32.596′, 450m) walk 20m left along the roadway to more steps and then along a level path heading towards giant plane trees.

1.30 At a spring the path turns down to a **roadway**, which leads over a bridge and past the dilapidated barracks of the mine workers. Rising up behind is the ropeway's reversing station, which one could examine by taking the path leading up left. A little later you reach the asphalt road.

> ***Alternative:*** The stony path to the emery mines described below calls for a degree of surefootedness. Instead one could go down the road to the right from here and dispense with the mines.

1.40 The road runs to the left and in one minute up to a **left-hand bend** (**P4:** N37°06.169′/E25°32.856′, 365m). At the sign "Azalas" begins the rather bumpy path, which soon leads past the cavernous mines. These were operated until 1990, the chutes for the emery boulders are still there [1] (see p.104).

1.55 Later you descend to the **by-road**, go 100m right and left down the road.

1

2

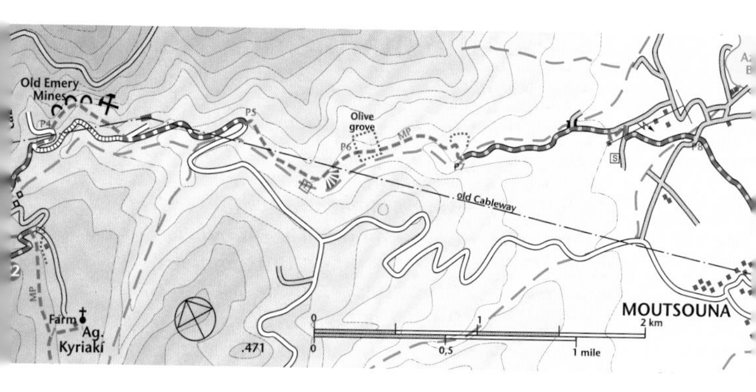

About 100m after passing under the ropeway, the road

2.10 makes a **sharp turn** to the right (**P5:** N37°05.916'/ E25°33.584', 210m). The path which begins here is easier

2.20 to walk on. Later, after a left-hand bend: **sea view!**

2.30 Shortly afterwards you stride through a walled **olive grove** (**P6:** N37°05.669'/E25°33.953') and proceed on the same level towards the sea. Going right, you traverse a

2.45 walled field with a house and come to a **roadway** (**P7:** N37°05.496'/E25°34.323', 80m). This leads in the direction of the sea, on the left Donoússa appears.

2.55 Disregard a bridge; at a **container** turn off to the left. After the first house (right, with power cables) you turn to the right. Before reaching the solar sails you descend left into the valley and, at the junction there (**P8:** N37° 05.188'/ E25°35.211'), straight ahead and over a hilltop to

3.20 **Moutsoúna.** The ropeway ends here; tons of emery boulders lie strewn around. The cranes for loading the ships still exist too. But above all there are plenty of pleasant harbour inns! 2.

If there is no bus, it is best to walk up to the main road in three minutes before hitch-hiking home.

23 Through the marble quarries of Kinídaros

This downhill hike of 4 hours follows country lanes in the interior of the island. First unspoilt rocky landscapes, then the largest marble quarries on Náxos. The kafenía in Kinídaros provide a good place to rest.
Marble factory, foray into the quarries.
■ 8 km, difference in altitude 320m, moderate

AWT
0.00 After just over an hour our bus reaches **Stavrós-Keramotí chapel** (**P1:** N37°06.362'/E25°31.512', 650m, see p.99 [1]), which stands alone in a saddle between Apíranthos and Kóronos. This is a request stop. Take the road running
0.10 *downhill* exactly opposite the entrance. In the **second sharp right-hand bend** go left into a roadway, which soon crosses a small bridge. On the right lies the valley of
0.25 Keramotí. Having reached the houses in **Kadís** [1], you find a marble table and a water tap.

You saunter down the roadway between gardens in a valley which down on the right broadens into an impressive, untouched rocky landscape [2]. A contrasting picture emerges after the following swing to the left – here man has taken possession of the rocks [3]. At a **fork**, (**P1:**
0.45 N37°05.976'/E29°29.801', 480m), where you go right, the old kalderími is visible under the roadway. In front of you lies a wide valley basin; dropping down into it, you soon
0.55 come to the road. On the right, is a **marble factory.** The workers are pleased to give hikers a glimpse of their work.

In the factory marble blocks are sawn into slabs which are then worked into door lintels, windowsills and floor tiles. Almost all the marble extracted on Náxos originates here.

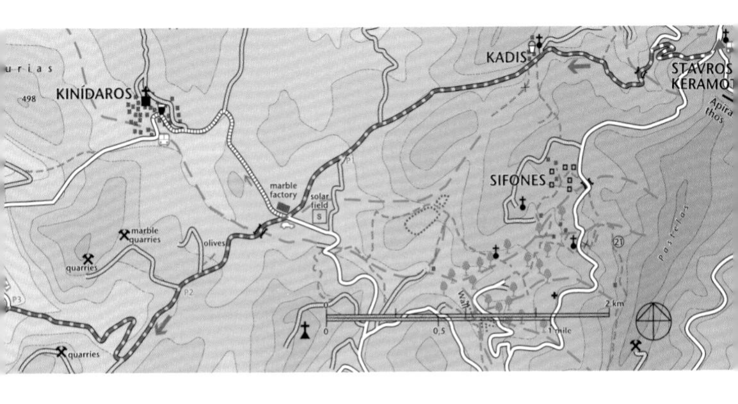

Shortcut: A 5 min. walk along the road to the right brings you to Kinídaros with well, kafenía and bus stop (irregular service).

Slightly to the right you follow the dusty roadway to the quarries. Should a truck drive by, it is wise to stay on the windward side. After a bridge the track, concreted at this point, starts climbing. Visible on the right is Kinídaros. Beyond the knoll one is amazed to look down into a dip covered with olive trees lying below the first marble quarry. For reasons of security it is of course forbidden to enter the bustling quarries. After an ascent the path **forks** (**P2:** N37°05.433'/E25°28.895', 430m). Staying on the same level, we go left towards the largest of the quarries and catch sight of Páros out at sea, the source of the finest marble in antiquity; it is translucent to a thickness of 35mm! Nowadays, though, the island no longer has any marble industry to speak of.

1.10

We are now standing in the midst of the largest stone quarries on Naxos, where marble has been extracted for 5,000 years.

Today the stone is extracted in steps of six meters in height. Two holes of about three and nine meters are drilled horizontally at right angles in the ground; they meet in the middle. Then the future block is horizontally prised out of the mountainside at the bottom with a cable saw. Then a vertical hole of six meters is drilled into the back edge. Again using the cable saw, a block of about 9 x 6 x 3

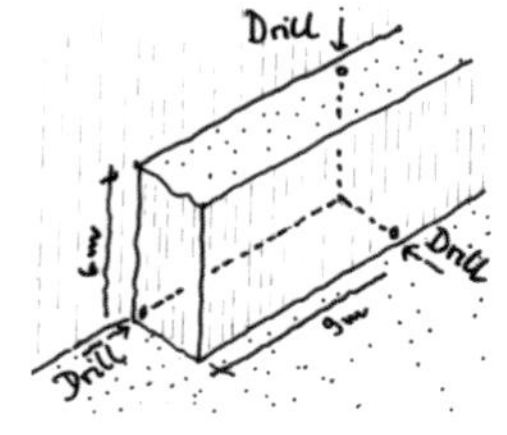

meters is prised out of the rock by means of two vertical cuts. This is sawn into smaller blocks on the spot before being hauled away.

A few meters before reaching the blocks spread out on the

1.20 slope **we turn off right** and descend into the valley on precious marble chippings between marble mountains 4. Again and again we cannot help peering up the mountainside to make sure nothing is rolling down …

1.40 On the **road** (**P3:** N37°05.384'/E25°28.055', 330m) we go left and try to wave down a car or the afternoon bus from Kinídaros. Otherwise it is still quite a slog along asphalt. However the fields in the hollow on the right are a pretty sight. As is the view back up to the enormous marble quarry!

2.05 The bus into town leaves from the **sign "Kouros"** near a Paraskeví chapel.

It is also possible to walk a few meters down left from here, then follow ③ to Kournochóri and catch the bus there beside the inn.

㉔ The Náxos crossing

This is the right trip for those who do not want to see any people for 5 to 6 hours and who do not need kafenía or chapels today. The very lovely hike mainly follows mule tracks marked "12" and cleared in 2016 . The initially fertile, later magnificently barren landscape possesses a romantic spring.
While it is possible to reach the starting point by bus, it is necessary to order a taxi on the way back (15 km, 22–25 €). Usually a nice driver will stop.
above Keramotí, turning place near the waterfalls, total 2 hours
■ *12 km, difference in altitude 620m, moderate to difficult*

AWT
0.00 Five kilometres beyond Apíranthos the **Stavrós-Keramotí chapel** [1] stands alone on the road (650m). This is where you alight and follow the vanishing bus for another 30m. At the end of the concrete retaining wall (left) you go down left and immediately through a gate. For 100m the path is rather slaty, but later easier to walk on,
0.10 before it finishes at the **road** to Keramotí [2]. Go down it for four minutes as far as a house (right, 40m before a mini-chapel), where you find the continuation of the path
0.15 on the left down to **Keramotí** car park.
0.20 30m beyond the **church** (475m) you go down left and 10m beyond a well come to the concrete steps beside a gully running out of the valley. Ignoring a left-turn, you
0.25 arrive at a **bridge** in the shady valley (**P1:** N37°06.609'/ E25°30.830'). Ascending out of the valley, you go straight ahead on the same level at a fork and follow the arrow "Waterfall". A delightful path leads you along the hillside through splendid rock formations. Be sure to take in the

beautiful view back towards Keramotí!

0.40 After a little stone **bridge** (**P2:** N37°06.864/ E25°30.377′),

0.50 a walled **wine-garden** (left) lies in a saddle. 3 min. later the "Waterfall" sign points down left (**P3:** N37°06.984′/

!! E25°30.048′, 440m). Here you go *straight ahead!*

Down to the left a descent of a few minutes would bring you to the **Routsoúna Waterfall** (**P4:** N37° 06.954′/ E25°29.950′). The "waterfall" is modest and the inviting paddling pool next to it has already been discovered by the agile turtles!

From here hire car drivers amble along the same lovely route back to **Keramotí.**

Trail "12" proceeds from **P3** above a rock-protected goat-pen (left) further to large plane trees ③ standing in a dip

1.00 below a spring next to a **rivulet** (**P5:** N37°07.075′/ E25°30.023′, 410 m). A romantic spot to rest.

1.10 From here on the path climbs in serpentine bends. **At the top** (**P6:** N37°07.138′/E25°29.723′) you saunter along for over half an hour more or less constantly at an altitude of 500m. To the left you see the marble mountains of Kinídaros, later, down in the valley, the Agios Artémios church with three naves concealed between trees (p 24).

1.50 **Two prominent rocks** ④ (**P7:** N37°07.385′/ E25°28.997′, 530 m) make the path narrower before it runs across an elevation. In the

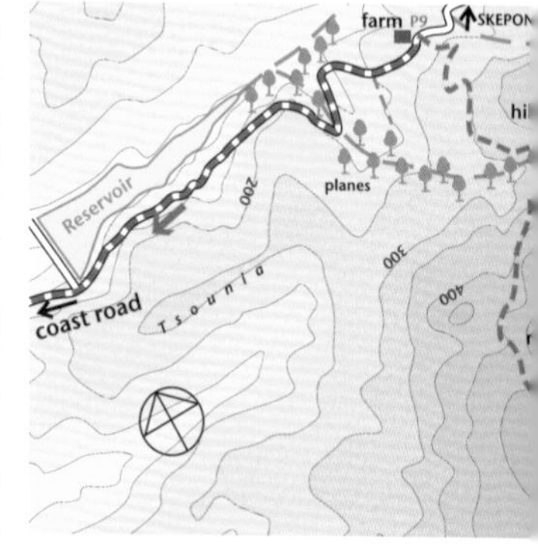

saddle you go right, past a group of rocks, and then downhill through a bizarre area with white marble blocks. Later there is a ditch down on the left of the now almost level rocky path. After a brief descent the mule track swings right and in a wide arc to a bush-covered ditch (**P8:** N37°07.928′/E25°29.393′, 390m). The path starts climbing again; concealed on the right is the **Agía Sortíra chapel.**

2.25

2.40 Having walked round the hill on the right-hand side, **you see** on an outcrop the few ruined houses of the deserted hamlet Skepóni. Serpentine bends lead down through rocks towards a sizeable agricultural enterprise.

In the valley below Skepóni you pass through a wire mesh gate and walk left along the **roadway** (**P9:** N37°08.340′/E25°29.229′, 225m). Proceeding through a **dip with planes** beside the stream course and later along the reservoir, you arrive at the **coast road** (30m). Now you only have to make a friendly face and jump into the first car that stops and you have already saved the taxi-fare!

2.50
3.05
3.35

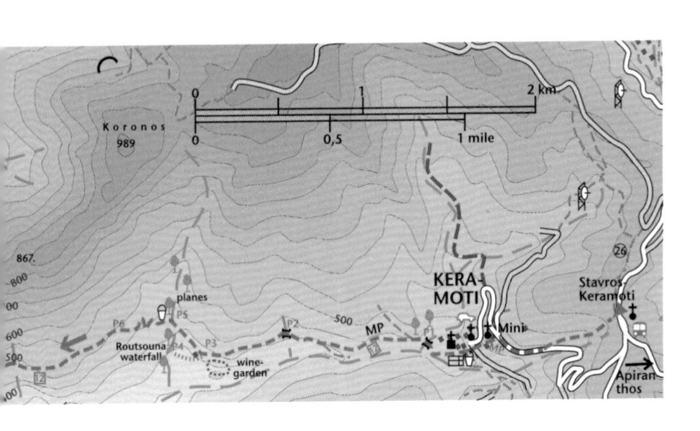

㉕ Panorama path to Liónas

Surely one of the most beautiful hikes on Náxos: In 4 hours almost entirely on clearly identifiable paths through charming landscapes. Some inns, but unfortunately no reliable wells.
It is necessary to organise the return journey from Liónas. The two landlords now offer to drive their guests back up to Kóronos (see below).
Kóronos
■ ***7km, difference in altitude 560m, moderate – difficult***

AWT 0.00 From the **bus stop in Kóronos** (with bronze bust) you descend 200m to the car park and opposite on down Mandiláras alley. It is named after the resistance fighter whose bust stands further up. He was murdered at the time of the military junta.

Five metres beyond the impressive church (left) proceed right on the same level, beneath three arches and down to

0.05 the plátsa, which has two inns. With the covered well behind you, you walk down to the left (not towards the inn “Dalas”), at the following fork right and across a small bridge. Then you proceed up left, right in front of a building with an outside staircase and after 15m left. Soon you

0.10 reach a concrete **path** and stroll along, envied by others, [1], beneath trees.

0.15 Later, on the wayside, is a terraced **garden** (left), where a vehicle track begins. 80m beyond this garden you leave

!! the vehicle track *by going left* on to a path (**P1:** N37° 07.216'/E25°32.516'). It leads you into the green valley and down right at an indistinct fork. Soon you traverse a

★ small stone bridge (**P2:** N37°07.987'/ E25°22.275') and amble on in the shade of planes [2]. The water of the pret-

ty looking stream is unfortunately polluted by the village. The trail broadens, it is possible to see further into the distance. Later you trek left above the

0.35 green valley. Go through a **gate**, then in front of a wall down

0.45 right to a **stone bridge** [3] and a roadway.

Having walked 200m up this, you traverse a closed-off goat pen. Five minutes later you turn off sharply down to the left (**P3:** N37°07.877'/E25°33.372') and

1.00 then reach a **concrete bridge.** Three minutes later the roadway ends after a gate (**P4:** N37° 07.989'/E25°33.518', 175m). Now you go up left through the rocks to a stepped path, which climbs steeply.

1.15 **At the top,** from a height of 250m, you have a wonderful view across the valley; on the opposite side you can make out mineshafts. Emery has been mined here since antiquity. The foundations of the supply cableway can still be seen against the rocks where a park for industrial history is going to be created (see below).

At an altitude of about 200m you walk towards the sea [4], un-

1.35 til you meet the **concrete track** which comes down from Mési (**P5:** N37°08.241'/E25°34.352'). Here you go down to the right, and again at the fork after three minutes. A little later

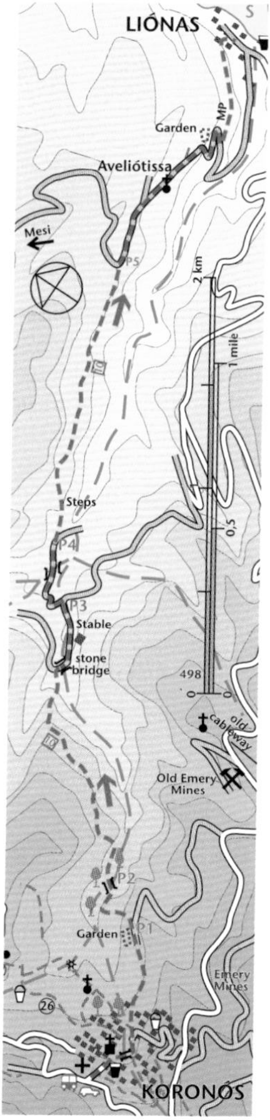

1.40 **Afdeliótissa chapel** lies just below the roadway, the entrance to the pretty picnic spot is a few metres further on. After 200m the track makes a serpentine and later a sharp

!! right-hand bend. 30m after that, *on the left,* begins a rather bumpy path, which brings you to the pebble beach

1.55 of **Liónas.**

A lot has happened here in the last few years – holiday houses, inns and hire cars: One of the latter may give us a lift back. And the two landlords offer to drive their guests up for free (taverna *Ntoyzenia:* 22850-51608, *Delfinaki:* -51290). You should however be up on the road shortly after 4.00 pm, when the bus from Apóllonas drives past.

Emery mining in Kóronos

Emery has been mined in the Kóronos valley since the Bronze Age. It is a very heavy, reddish-brown conglomerate consisting of magnetite, mica und corundum which is embedded in marble. It is almost as hard as diamond and is used as an abrasive.

The state-owned mines flourished economically in the 1920s, giving employment to as many as one thousand miners from all over the region. Mining was stopped around 1990, as nowadays emery is almost entirely manufactured synthetically. Today the mines are only worked sporadically in order to finance the miners' insurance. Some of the mines can still be visited. Also still standing are the pylons of the supply cableway which runs down to the port of transhipment, Moutsoúna in the next valley further south ㉒. To commemorate this bygone era, work has begun on the construction of a technical open-air museum. An older museum can be found on the road to Liónas.

㉖ The Kóronos valley

The 2-hour hike, almost entirely without shade, leads down wide paved paths to the picturesque village of Kóronos on the slopes and on up through vineyards to the well-nigh deserted Skadó. A nice alternative would be to start the tour in Kóronos instead and then extend it in Skadó by using tour 27 (see below).
Stávros or Pórta, bus back to the car (2 €).
Or round-trip below Kóronos.
■ *3 km, difference in altitude 180m, easy-moderate*

AWT
0.00 The bus has a request stop at **Stavrós-Keramotí** chapel (650m, 1 p. 99). (But one could also alight 4 min. later at "Pórta".)

Standing beside the road 100m beyond the chapel is a ΔEH power pole. There, parallel with the road, begins a
0.10 gravel trail. At the top you take the **roadway** down right and the road left up to the saddle (715m). This is also
0.15 called "**Pórta**", the portal to Kóronos. On the left a well-preserved kalderimi leads you away from the road and down into the valley 1.

With a view of Kóronos and Skadó you walk downhill and
0.25 later across the **road** (**P1:** N37°06.669'/E25°32.009'). On the far side concrete steps take you on down, but after one minute we like the natural steps on the left at the fork better 2. They lead to a small bridge, thence with a concrete
0.30 pavement. Go right at the **fork** (**P2:** N37°06.939'/E25° 32.084', 570m) and then down the painted alleys to the
0.35 tranquil **plátsa of Kóronos** 3. Shady inns next to the well await your arrival ...

Alternative: At **Kóronos bus stop** drop 200m to the car park and on down the alley on the far side.

1

2

Five meters beyond the large St. Marina church covered with stone tiles (left) stroll right on the same level, through three arches to the **plátsa.**

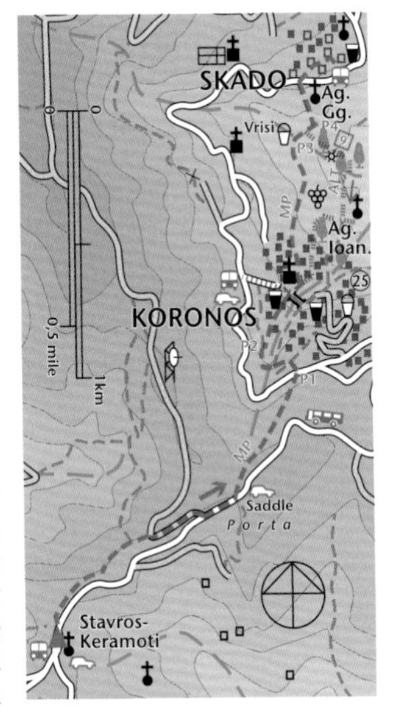

0.35 From the **plátsa** you ascend to the right of the well and, at the end of the alley with three arches, to the large St. Marina church (left). Below the church square (left, with seating steps) the alley runs past the panorama café *Perasma* (right) on the same level. At a power pole (and a well on the left) bear half-right and down four steps. Then down right at a metal gate, before leaving the village on concrete steps. A beautiful path [4] winds its way down through vines, which suffered a little from the bush fire in 2017.

In the valley bottom you traverse the watercourse at a

0.50 **pumping station** (Vrisí) (**P3:** N37°07.371'/E25°32.135', 480m) and climb uphill.

Round trip: Just beyond the pumping station go down into the valley on the right beside a large white metal sign marking the trail "9". Passing a water basin, you again traverse the watercourse. The climb back up on the far side starts with serpentine bends. Higher up, at

3

4

the second metal sign, a detour leads left to the wonderfully situated **St. John's chapel.** Returning on the main trail, you take a wide leftward curve back up to the plátsa in **Kóronos** (AWT from Vrisí 25 min.)

0.50 !! After an ascent of six minutes you branch off *up left immediately after a metal sign* (**P4:** N37°07.475'/E25°32.242') and, on concrete steps, pass the small St. George's church with elegant marble iconostasis.

1.00 Shortly afterwards you cross the road and walk up between the houses in **Skadó** (550m). The village is almost deserted, 15 inhabitants are said to still live here. Sometimes noises can be heard behind the doors. The many ruins bear testimony to better times, when the menfolk found work in the emery mines. At least there is an inn on the road where you wait for the bus!

Sporty types, on the other hand, turn their energies to tour 27.

Feast-Days – Panigíri

Often the hiker is fortunate enough to land completely unexpectedly in the middle of a religious festival.

The church or chapel is bedecked with flags, a large congregation of guests in festive dress is sitting around – in their midst at least one priest. The tables are groaning under the weight of the food which the womanfolk or the owner of a private chapel have brought with them. Homemade drinks are proffered; canned drinks are sold at cost price. Immediately the stranger is invited to taste the many dishes and is involved in a conversation. These are unforgettable Greek moments.

The festivals take place on the name day of the patron saint of the church involved:

Date	Feast	Date	Feast
23rd April	Ayios Geórgios	20th Juli	Profítis Ilías
5th Mai	Ayía Iríni	26th Juli	Ayía Paraskeví
21st Mai	Ayios Konstantínos	27th Juli	Ayios Panteleímon
Ascension Day	Ayía Análipsi	6th August	Metamórphosis
Whitsuntide	Ayía Triáda	15th August	Assumption of the Virgin
24th Juni	A. Ioánnis Pródomos	29th August	Ayios Ioánnis
29th Juni	Ayii Apóstoli	1st Sept.	Ayios Mámas
7th Juli	Ayía Kyriakí	14th Sept.	Ayios Stavrós

㉗ A shady path for hot days

Trekking almost entirely along rural paths and in the shade of large trees, you reach the mountain village of Koronída in the north of Naxos in 2½ hours. Springs and tavernas make this a perfect tour.
Those who prefer a longer trek can already start in Kóronos ㉖.
Skadó or Kóronos, bus back to the car
■ *5 km, difference in altitude 150m, moderate*

AWT
0.00 The bus stops at the only inn in **Skadó.** Huddled above it are the deserted houses occupied by a mere fifteen inhabitants. On the north side of the village the road forks - we walk left up the hill. Just beyond the second right-hand bend, on the left next to a wooden board marked "9", are steep stone steps. The rather dilapidated zigzag bends which then follow are hard to discern in places.

0.15 But further up are accompanying **walls** on the left and right, between which tall grass grows. Then comes a group of trees (**P1:** N37°07.848'/E25°32.270'). Thereafter the ascending path becomes wider, permitting the hiker to enjoy the romantic wildness of the landscape on the right. On these hillsides emery is still mined sporadically in winter (see p.104).

!! 250m beyond the group of trees you should remember to heed a *vertically placed* **stone slab**, which marks the
0.20 branch-off down right. From this path you can soon see the antenna – our interim destination [1].

0.30 Go left 40m on the road, turn off to the right and walk past the **antenna** (right 650m). On the roadway you pro-
0.40 ceed left down to a **turning place** (**P2:** N37°08.201'/ E25°32.272').

1

2

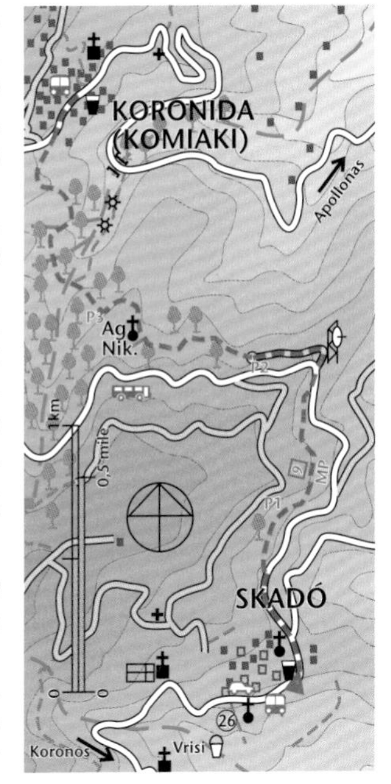

Here begins a well-maintained and shady path. On the slopes to the right is the village of Koronída and visible out at sea is Apóllonas.

0.50 40m beyond a **water basin** (left) you go right at the fork (and left to the old St. Nicolas chapel.) The trail becomes wider for a short while, but then drops and is difficult to negotiate due to mossy stones. After a

1.00 gate comes a short **level stretch** (**P3:** N37°08.343'/ E25°31.800', 535m).

Not far beyond this the path forks (to watermills on the right).

Proceed left and across a stream. After a further descent comes another

1.05 **stream** (500m). But then you stride proudly up through plane trees and walls to

1.20 **Koronída** [2], also designated by its second name **Komiakí** in the bus timetables. Bus tickets can be bought further down on the right in the taverna *Internet* – and something to wet your whistle too.

28 The unfinished god

After the bus journey through the mountains of Náxos you wander for 3½ hours along a gently downhill incline to the huge, unfinished monumental statue of Apóllonas. The bus timetable allows 4½ hours for the tour. Tavernas are available at the beginning and end of the hike.

Koronída, with bus back to the car

■ *7 km, difference in altitude 570m, easy to moderate*

AWT Unless you are in the mood to celebrate the exciting bus journey on the terrace of the kafeníon *Internet* at the bus
0.00 stop in **Koronída** (aka **Komiakí**), walk up the steps diagonally opposite and into the village (570m). Once there,
!! stroll round the churchyard (right) before proceeding *up*
0.05 *left* at the **fork** after 80m – after the furrowed plane tree. A new paved path and yellow arrows eventually lead to a
0.10 **Mycenean burial chamber.**

The subterranean chamber dates from the 15th century BC. The hive-like structure measuring 3½m in width was erected for a chieftain and is one of the best-preserved graves on the Cyclades.

Return along the same path, but going down the steps before the first houses! After 30m a "9" on the left marks the mule track which meanders beautifully through the ter-
0.20 raced vineyards 1 and a cluster **of oak trees.**
Where the paths intersect (**P1:** N37°08.895'/E25°32.073'),
0.30 you walk up left. Passing a **shelter** for goats, you continue 40m along a roadway (**P2:** N37°09.202'/ E25°32.386', 470m). After the branch-off to the left the easily discernible, slaty track runs between small spurge bushes.
0.45 A little **picnic bench** affords a good vantage point. Fur-

ther down you are joined by a fence on the right. The track then becomes a wide kalderími which, hugging a
1.10 long **farmstead** on the right (house 304) (**P3:** N37°09.689'/E25°32.745', 230m), heads towards the sea. After a few zig-zags you turn off right through a gate at the fork above a group of houses. Shortly afterwards
1.25 you drop left to the **road** and then up right as far as the right turn.

Here a concrete track leads left down into a shady, green valley. At the left branch-off you keep straight ahead
1.35 despite the blackberries! After a **water mill** (left) at the bottom of the valley (**P4:** N37°09.906'/E25°33.178') your route runs beneath plane trees back up to the road, which drops slightly.
1.40 At the **fork**, go up left for 6 min. The
1.45 sign "Koúros" guides you left to the steps which lead to the more than 10 metre high **marble statue** ②.
1.55 *On account of the beard it is assumed to be a statue of* ***Diónysos.*** *Hence it is no "koúros", no youth, but a god.*

Due to several material defects the statue was never completed. The poor god has therefore been lying in an uncomfortable, oblique position in a former quarry for 2,500 years.

Back on the road you go left and, 80m further down, descend to the right. Then, after a short stretch, you take the footpath on
2.00 the right down to **Apóllonas.** Here you run into large crowds of tourists who have come by bus for a quick meal in one of the restaurants set up to cater for them. On the terrace of the *Kaliméra* one can expect food that is prepared with greater care.

A minibus brings you back up to Koronída, where the big bus is already waiting.

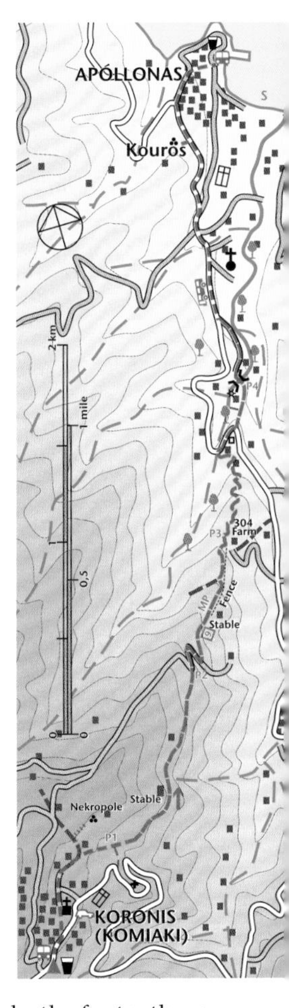

SMALL CYCLADES LINES

Small Cyclades

Between Náxos and Amorgós are several small islands for visitors who would like to be transported back to the beginnings of tourism - individual travellers who would like to experience the genuine Greek lifestyle, prefer to stay in private guesthouses instead of holiday residences and enjoy exploring islands on foot. For them the Small Cyclades are an ideal destination.

Μικρές Κυκλάδες

These islands were also called "Erimonísia" – "Lonely Islands". Because pirates used the bays as hideouts, they were deserted for centuries. Not until the foundation of Greece in 1832 did settlers return.
The archipelago consists of twenty small and six large islands, only four of which are inhabited though.
The popular bathing island *Koufonísi* offers a string of long sandy beaches and small coves on the east side. The range of tourist hotels and tavernas is hence much greater than on the neighbouring islands *Donoússa, Iráklia* and *Schinoússa*. There the facilities are more basic, but the opportunities for hiking much better. The first two afford partly very challenging tours, albeit with the prospect of discovering nice bathing coves.
Island maps are offered by Anavasi on the rear side of the Naxos map. Skaï and Orama have their own maps of the Small Cyclades.
It is easy to reach these islands from Náxos: with the faithful, slightly shaky "Skopelítis" (left). "Landlubbers" may encounter problems on the upper deck during rough sea passages. During the season it is in service between Náxos and Amorgós every workday. Donoússa, however, is only served three times a week.
Those who like the old ways, do not mind choosing their dishes in the kitchen and wish to frequent cosy inns with the locals and just a few other guests should not miss a short sojourn over here with the help of the "Skopelitis"!

Donoússa

The northernmost, most remote and windiest of the "Small Cyclades" is mountainous and almost treeless, although it has several springs. Not overrun by tourists, the island is annually frequented by a faithful group of regulars who like to meet at *To Kýma* near the harbour. While the *Skopelítis* only calls in three times a week, (p.131), ferries stop more often. Unfortunately the popular former mule track round the island has been partly destroyed by the road. The hike described below follows the remains of the old track and again makes it possible to do the beautiful island circular tour. The road does however facilitate a helpful private bus service!
A taxi can be ordered at 0030-6932-488529.

㉙ Tour of the island

The 6 to 7-hour trek leads over a 230m high ridge to the wide bay of Kalotarítissa. After a further 25-minute ascent along the road it proceeds round the island; the hike follows mule tracks and dirt tracks. There are wells and taverns.
The ascent to Mersíni could be curtailed by taking the bus!
■ 15 km, difference in altitude 2 x 250m, difficult

AWT
0.00 We begin in **Agios Stávros** 1 below the **village church** Tímios Stávros, go right past the fountain at the post office and shortly afterwards at the next fountain left up the steps! A roadway takes us in a northerly direction and
0.07 across the **road.** Pass the "windmill" on your left, it is part of a house which unites a mixture of styles from different

epochs and continents in bad taste. At a builder's yard (right) begins the path "1".

Slowly we wander along a wide mule track on the left-
0.15 hand side of a streambed to an isolated **pine tree** to the
0.25 right of a hill [2] Having crossed a **dry-bed** and a dirt track diagonally to the right, we join a wide dust track higher up for 13 min. Up to the right are abandoned mines.

0.40 But before **the roadway zigzags begin**, we find the old path again. Later, 20m over to the right, it traverses the
0.45 track and leads up to a windy **pass** (230m) north of Mount Papás. Where the dust track ends, the continuation of the path comes into view again. Looking down over the protected bay [3] in a wide right bend, we skirt alongside the cliffs and proceed in zigzags down into the still un-
1.10 spoilt hamlet of **Kalotarítissa.**

In 1914, at the beginning of the First World War, an armed conflict almost erupted in this tranquil bay. Two German cruisers met here, undiscovered, for one whole day to take on coal from a German supply ship. At sea the Royal Navy was searching for them, Greece was still neutral. But the local shepherds evidently didn't have any connection with the outside world so as to relay the discovery. Or they just didn't know that war had broken out … The German vessels then continued their journey to allied Turkey.

Shortcut: The bus could take you up to Mersíni.

1.15 We could take a break at either of two **beaches** or at the *Mitsos* taverna. Then, 30m beyond the road bridge, we continue left along a descending roadway. This runs plea-
1.25 santly along the coastline to a little **walled garden** (behind it is a source) (**P1:** N36°52.014'/E25°31.582'), before
1.35 which we turn left up to the **road.**

1

2

Seven minutes later a power line crosses overhead; 150m
1.45 beyond that, at a **cistern** (right), (**P2:** N37°06.673′/E25° 49.599′, 180m), you leave the road by going right. Climbing left below the fence, you find another cistern, above which a monopáti runs until ending at the road again.
2.00 After a wide **right bend** at the apex of the hike (250m),
2.10 the road reaches **Mersíni.** There you descend the steep concrete track and, at the bottom above the right-hand bend, find the very pleasant panorama inn *Tzi-Tzi.* Short break?

If you prefer spring water: Five minutes further down, after a left turn, is the romantic **spring** *(pigí)* 4.

2.20 From *Tzi-Tzi* you walk up in the same direction to **the bus** stop. (On the left the isolated Sophia Chapel). From there you go inland on the road and, after about 100m, you find down left the old mule track again.
This goes round the valley on the level below the road with views of the rich farmland. Above it the ruin of the "Upper Mill" – *Páno Mýlos,* which worked until the 1970ies.
Shortly after a fork in the path, where you have gone right (**P3:** N37°06.019′/E25°49.124′, 190m), you go diagonally
2.45 left across the **road** and now proceed above it. Later descending left over marble boulders into the side valley you
2.50 rejoin the **road** and go downhill. After 80m steps marked "3" go up right and, 60m further up, lead above the ham-
2.55 let **Messaría.** Almost deserted today, it was the island's chorá until 1970. There was the blacksmith's workshop and the charcoal plant for the needs of the island.
At the fork beyond that we continue right/straight on, first on the same level and then downhill in curves which afford distant views. That is how the entire path used to

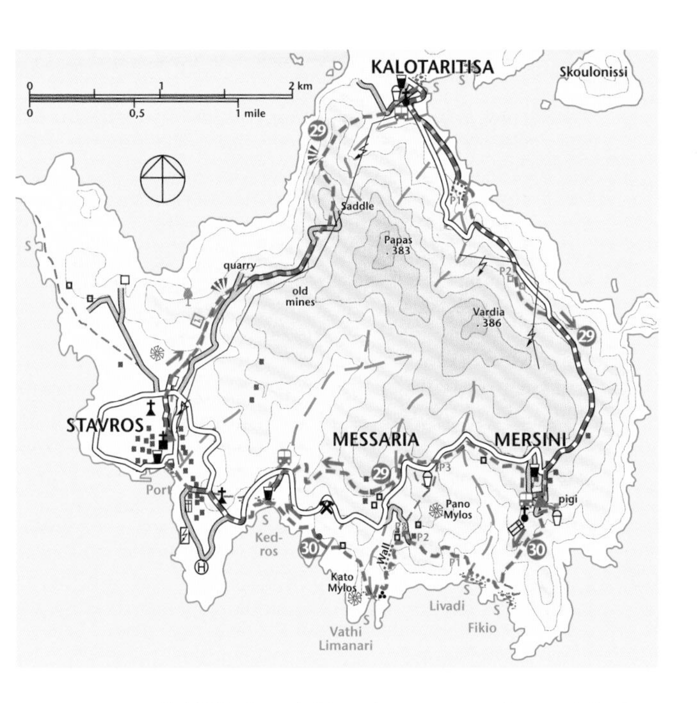

run until 1997. On a hilltop it peters out for a while, but later, on the right, runs on down into the valley. Having crossed the road, you arrive at **Kédros strand** and treat yourself to a cool drink in the beach bar. From there you take the paved path to the right over a crest and on to the road to **Stávros.**

3.15

3.30

Living with a view of Stávros

Prassinos Studios offer good sunset views across the beach and the harbour, see p. 115. *prassinosstudios@gmail.com*

30 The windmill strand

The former principal place Messariá had two windmills, the upper one and the lower one. Today the remains will serve us as an aid to orientation. The idyllic 3 to 4-hour trek follows easily identifiable trails along the coast. Swimming gear is not necessarily required.
Off we go – a laid-back beach bar awaits us!
■ 5 km, difference in altitude 145m, moderate
▷ *Map see previous page*

AWT
0.00
0.04 From **Mersíni** bus stop descend the steep concrete track and turn off half-right on to the paved track. Then, further down at the fork, left and down to the **spring**, Greek *pigí* (p. 116, 4). Water babbles beneath a giant plane tree the whole year round, as gold fish have also noticed.
!! Go back uphill again and *after 30m left,* past the former solar panel system, until you find the path "2" going down left. Keeping to the right there, you end up at the
0.10 beautiful **sandy bay of Livádi** 1. Some of the guests
★ have made themselves at home, bathing gear is frowned upon.

On the far side of Livádi Bay, to the left of the ditch, a well-beaten track runs uphill for about 3 min. towards the "upper windmill". At a transverse wall the track swings left and runs in the direttissima up to a further, transverse
0.30 **retaining wall** (**P1:** N37°06.023'/E25°49.116'). Here you
!! continue *60m to the right on the same level,* then again up left in the direttissima until where the track runs horizontally. On the left the terrain falls away to the sea, down on a peninsula stands the "lower windmill" – that's where we're heading! Beyond these the Small Cyclades, framed by Amorgós and Náxos, seem to be swimming in a large

1

2

lake. Proceeding round the hill you come to a house, be-
0.40 side which a **roadway** ends (**P2:** N37°05.658′/E25° 49.000′, 120m). Take this to walk round a dip in a left-hand arc until, after 200m, a ruin with partly collapsed roof blocks the way (**P3:** N37°05.713′/E25° 48.933′). At the fence you turn off left at right-angles, pass after 30m through the deserted farm and, in the same direction, three terraced cornfields too. At the lower edge of the field are cairns. They guide you to the left of a long wall through the open terrain towards a rocky headland, where in 1967 a settlement from the Geometric Period was discovered. Opposite lies the promontory with the "lower windmill" (Káto Mýlos). In zigzags you descend
0.55 right to the **Bay of Vathí Limenari** (**P4:** N37°05.483′/ E25°48.821′).

The large, partly lava and marble stones do not bother us – between the walls of the former boatshed soft, fine sand invites us to take a prolonged break.

In the Geometric Period (10th–7th century B.C.) the bay afforded an important anchorage place for the merchant vessels. The settlement on the peninsula to the left consisted of 12 rectangular buildings, protected by a defensive wall – a rarity in those times. The buildings were two-spaced with flat roof. A large part of the settlement appears to have sunken in the sea. The Archeological Museum in Náxos keeps the ceramic finds, mostly vessels and cooking utensils.

It is hard to drag ourselves away from this place. On the far side of the bay, 40m from the strand, you find the continuation of path "4" leading uphill. First you spot the houses and ruins of Messariá up right, then, on the
1.05 **saddle** with the dilapidated windmill, the twin chapel of the Panagía as well.

About 100m removed from the sea, the path heads in this direction between sea and road ②. You traverse a channel (**P5:** N37°05.705′/E25°48.618′) and end up, as planned,
1.25 on the fine sand of **Kédros.**

The nudes get quite a surprise when they behold hikers in boots. In the popular beach bar we can finally enjoy the promised drink – reclining in a deck chair of course. Or maybe even two, for we already know the way back to
1.40 **Stavrós.**

Iraklià

This mountainous island has managed to retain something of its former charm. In the cosy tavernas in Agios Geórgios one mainly encounters regular guests who want to spend a couple of quiet days here. And the island has a couple of uncrowded beaches to offer too.
Iraklià is suitable for trekking because quite a few of the old mule tracks still exist and are mostly marked. They are partly quite strenuous. In the supermarket at the harbour you can enquire whether the taxi-boat "Anemos" might shorten hike 31.

31 The cave of the Cyclops?

For the most part following paths, the 6 to 7-hour trek leads to the cave of St. John and back again in a wide arc.
A torch or a cigarette lighter is useful for the cave.
The taxi-boat makes it possible to shorten the way.
■ 14 km, difference in altitude 285m, difficult

AWT
0.00
0.05

At the freestanding **Taxiárchis Church** at the top end of **Agios Geórgios** you leave the village on a concrete and, later, dirt track and pass a **chapel of St. John** (left). (On the right a path leads to Voriní bay with two caves.)

0.15

After three minutes you go straight ahead at the left branch-off to a vineyard, at the next major **fork** with signpost (**P1:** N36°51.227'/E25°27.598') again straight on up the dirt track. (The kalderími on the left is used on the following tour.) You are guided by a wall on the left, al-

lowing you to devote yourself to the outlook over Páros
0.25 and Náxos. At the **turn-off to the left** (**P2:** N36°50.874'/E25°27.173', 120m) you stride straight on uphill and then, on the left of a chapel, along the old monopáti to
0.35 the deserted hamlet of **Athanássis.**

Having passed the three modest houses, you come, after the house at the top, to a gate and again to a monopáti,
0.40 which runs through a **ditch.** On the far side of this you climb rather steeply, first to the left of the wall and later on the right-hand side of a wall through juniper bushes
0.55 and rocks. Once up on the **Seládi ridge** (**P3:** N36°50.225'/E25°26.558', 285m) you use an opening through the wall and descend a path.

The newly created path runs along the hillside, affording a view of the next bay and Páros. You can regain your
1.10 breath in the shade of an isolated **pine.** Where a path turns off to the right two minutes later, you proceed
!! straight ahead and, at the next fork, *up left*. Shortly afterwards you find yourself in a hollow in front of the two
1.20 **Caves of Ágios Ioánnis**, but you do not actually see these until you are standing 10m in front of them 1. (**P4:** N36°49.727'/E25°26.199', 110m),

On the left is the large cave chamber where the big church festival takes place on 28th August, attracting the entire population of the island.

This is said to be the mythical cave of the Cyclopes, from which Odysseus and his followers, clinging beneath goats, are supposed to have escaped. However, the same is also claimed by the inhabitants of the island Lachea off the east coast of Sicily ….

On the right is a small cave with a bell at the entrance. If you light a few of the candles at the altar, you may be able to conjure up the atmosphere of the cave festivities.

Shortcut: The route described below affords fabulous views but – with a 25-minute ascent – is long. You could turn back here and at **P3** take the serpentine bends marked with "3" down to **Panagía**, AWT as far as there: 2.25.

1.20 The athletic hiker walks back from the **caves** and *down*
!! *left after the right-hand bend.* Then after 50m left on to trail "5" and through a ditch. Take the following ascent leisurely - not as hurriedly as Odysseus and his six remaining followers when pursued by the blinded Cyclops. Pylons of bricks are a good aid to orientation. Having passed
1.35 through a gap in the wall, you begin a **level panorama path** with stupendous views over to Ios, Páros and Náxos.
1.50 Later rocks on the right form a kind of **amphitheatre** (**P5:** N36°49.941'/E25°25.646'). A few rocks are missing – was it the Cyclops which hurled them down? The two crags in front of Alimniás bay are supposed to bear witness to the act. That is where Odysseus' ships are said to have laid up – according to the myth told by the locals (see below).
From here you descend and walk past a new shed (right). At the beginning of a wide, level saddle trail "5" *turns off*
!! *right!* (The pylon stands 10m to the right of the branch-off.) The return route commences.
Between phrýgana the brick-pylons ② guide us safely
2.15 down into the **ditch by the sea** (**P6:** N36°50.015'/E25°25.964'). Bathing is not possible though. The path continues on top of the rocky coastline, but now strangely enough marked "6". In front of an enclosed pen it runs left, through a gate. While still continuing on the same
2.30 level, beyond another gate the way **ascends**, only briefly interrupted by a ditch. Fairly high up the path swings right (**P7:** N36°50.671'/E25°26.266, 170m') – and climbs again.
2.55 However from the **elevation** (**P8:** N36°50.682'/E25° 26.468', 230m) you proudly look down at Agios Geórgios.
3.05 The path is now level, then descending to **Athanássis.** With a spring in your step you proceed further down to
3.40 **Àgios Geórgios.**

Alternative: If you care for a dip, walk right at **P2** as far as the road. Go left down it for 7 min. until you find a
3.45 dirt track on the right leading down to **Livadi beach.**

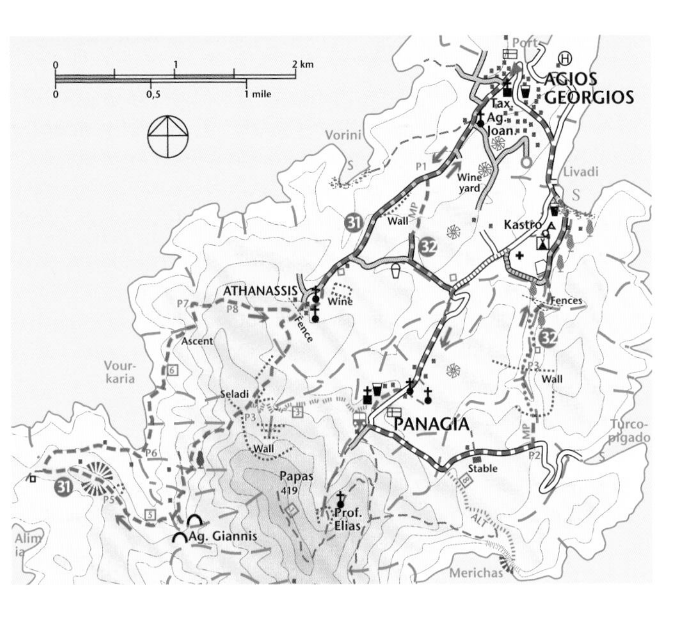

The Odyssey, as it is usually told

After Troy was destroyed, Odysseus journeyed with his 12 ships along *the Greek mainland* back to the island of Ithaca, off the coast of present-day Patras. But south of the Peloponnese a seven-day storm swept the ships to Djerba off the African coast. So they sailed north again and emerged off Sicily.

There they discovered, *from the ships,* a large cave. Although it was known that the inhabitants of the island were coarse, one-eyed fellows, Odysseus and twelve of his crew explored this cave but were surprised by the owner of the cave. He carefully closed the entrance with a rock and then ate two of the companions. The next day, the Cyclops had some business to do, ate two more men and closed his cave. Again in the evening, in reverse order. But Odysseus had noticed that the Cyclops was a milk drinker and offered him retsina. That helped. The giant fell over heavily drunk and they could blind his eye with a glowing stake. The rock at the entrance still remained. Since the goats had to be let out, the Greeks clung to the underbelly of the middle beast of the three-packs which the cunning Odysseus had previously bound together. The blind Cyclops, however, did not spot them when frisking the goats and pushed the rock away. Let's get out of here! The blind giant threw rocks at the ships, but didn't hit anything. He asked his father Poseidon, God of the Sea, to hinder Odysseus' journey. And so it came to pass…

㉜ Livádi strand

Λειβάδι – *Livadi, one of those Greek words that the visitor comes across on every island. It actually means a meadow, but here, as so often, also a large bathing beach.*
This strand is the crowning glory on a 3-hour hike along country lanes and one short stretch of road. With good orientation the trek ends on goat tracks, through partly unspoilt landscape.
■ *10 km, difference in altitude 160m, easy*
▷ *Map see previous page*

AWT The first section corresponds to the previous hike as far as
0.15 the **left turn-off** (**P1:** 36°51.227'/E25°27.598').
Here you turn up left on to an old kalderími. After the hill it descends to a cistern in the valley. Go left there to the
0.30 **road.**

> ***Shortcut:*** If you go left down the road for seven minutes and, at the sign "Kastro", take the roadway to the right into the valley, you come in just under 20 minutes to **Livádi strand.**

0.30 To the right it is about 50m to the old paved path, a short-
0.55 cut to the road leading to **Panagía** further up. There you then go right, up the village lane, past the nice panorama taverna "To Steki" on the right-hand side and, after the
1.00 large domed church, on to the **bus station** (with traffic mirror).
You walk a few steps on the level and past the right-hand turn-off (This is where the ascent to Mount Papas starts.) The road leads you into undulating farming country. Af-
1.10 ter a left bend in a dip, beside a field wall, a **signpost** points to the right.

1

2

Alternative: Following the sign to the right, you will find a pretty mule track, which you leave again to the right after ten minutes. After a further five minutes, latterly without a path, you arrive at the steep rock face which surrounds **Merichas Bay.** You cannot go down, but you can enjoy the view over a picnic.

1.10 The road leads us straight on past a big stable (right). At the turn-off of a path there we stay on the road. About 1.20 350m further, after a horizontal stretch of road, our **mule track** branches left (**P2:** N36°50.684'/E25°26.470') [1]. (Straight ahead would bring us to the shingle bay of Turcopigádo after ten minutes.)

The mule track is only about 100m long. Here we have to clamber over the fence on the right and then, right of centre, navigate our way through the juniper bushes. Although there is no path for the first few metres, Mt. Zeus on Náxos points the way for us. On the right, about 20-30m away, a ditch. Later goat tracks come into view. A dry-bed comes down from the left and widens the Pistikós 1.40 valley. Beyond that, the wall narrows to a **passage** (**P3:** N36°50.365'/E25°28.135').

Always remaining beside the gravel bed, we change sides a couple of times. The sea is nowhere to be seen in the rather unreal surroundings, but Mt. Zeus and later the ruins of the Venetian kástro on the hill show us the way. Having passed a cistern [2], we traverse an enclosure and beyond it find a country lane.

1.50 Lower down a **roadway** emerges from a side valley on the left; we continue straight on along this, soon passing a refuse dump (left). Then follows the camp site on the left, right below the kástro. We have soon reached our destina-2.00 tion: the wide sandy bay of **Livádi** with a beach tavern. Lying on the strand is so nice that we scarcely feel like climbing up through the undergrowth to the kástro. The castle still has foundation walls and the portal to a larger building.

It is along the road that we return, too, turning up left at 2.15 the fork and then down into the peace and quiet of **Agios Geórgios.** Already while sauntering downhill, we can choose which taverna to stop at for supper.

 Epáno Koufonísi, Loutrós Bay

Koufonísi

The island is actually called "Upper - Epáno" Koufonísi, as it is the northern, i.e. "upper" of two islands by the same name. While the "lower" one is uninhabited, this very small and flat isle has good tourist facilities. In August these are well filled by bathing guests who are attracted mostly by the long sandy beaches and rock formations.
Since the island, which has scarcely any trees, has only been inhabited again for the past 200 years, there are no dwellings outside the villages and no chapels.
It is possible to reach the lower, uninhabited "Káto Koufonísi" several times a day with Kaíkis. There one can do a beautiful coastal walk past several empty sandy beaches.

33 Round tour of the island

Almost entirely using level well-beaten tracks, this 4-hour tour through the interior of the island leads to the wide sandy bay of Porí. It returns back to the village past further sandy beaches.
Tavernas exist in Porí and Finíkas.
■ 8 km, difference in altitude 100m, easy

AWT From **St. George's Church** we take the alley running west
0.00 through the village, turning right at each of the two forks
0.05 and down to the **Loutró bay** with the picturesque shipyard (p. 126). On the left is Maria's sunset taverna *To Steki*.
0.10 Stroll past the ouzerie (left) over the hill to the **fishing harbour Parianós.**
In the middle of the harbour perimeter we veer right behind the inn with the three palms. At the electricity meter

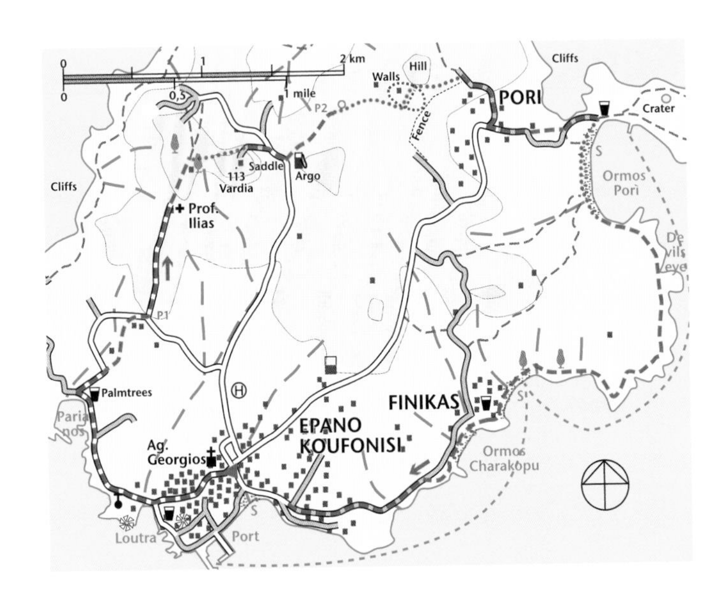

in the following left-hand bend we proceed straight on away from the concrete track and along wheel ruts through a field. Further up we turn right on the road, but branch up to the left after 100m (**P1:** N36°56.352'/E25° 35.794'). The surface becomes a dust track, to the right of which is a large, whitewashed **devotional square**, the remains of a Byzantine Profítis Elías chapel 1.

0.25

Further up the now indistinct path runs past a shed (right). Behind it we cross the field wall to the right and amble without a path towards Várdia hill, at 113m the island's highest point. Below the "peak" we come to a roadway, which ends further down to the left at a concrete track. We go up this to the right, but branch horizontal left below the Argo petrol station into a wall-lined monopáti, which however ends after 200m in front of a **wall** (**P2:** N36°56.834'/ E25°36.410').

0.50

On the far side, though, a wide track leads down to a round cistern. There, two meters higher up, we go right and saunter half-right in open terrain without a path, towards two small stone huts. The second hut, below the hill, stands in a large, walled **oval field.** In the middle (**P3:** N36°56.888'/E25°36.548') the field is divided by a further wall. It is easiest to traverse the oval by surmounting the outer walls here. A track then takes us on, about

1.00

30m above the fences of holiday houses, and reaches a roadway. Through a double gate it brings us down to the

1.20 broad, beautiful **sandy beach of Porí** with an airy, very popular inn.

Those who eschew the idea of taking the boat back proceed on the southern side of the strand through a field wall and, about 150m beyond it, come to a small plateau. A little lower down, overlooking the sea, lies a water-filled cave, which is called the "Devil's eye" – gazing out to the beautiful sea.

Continuing along the coast we stroll on a wide path, past

2.00 beautiful sandy beaches, to the hotel complex of **Finíkas.** There we can fortify ourselves in the shady beach taverna

2.15 for the last leg of the tour to **Chóra.**

■ Island hopping

The *Blue Star Ferries* sail from Piraeus, via Náxos (+ 6 hrs.) and the Small Cyclades to Amorgós.
www.bluestarferries.com

Several fast catamaran ferries from Piraeus, Mýkonos and Santorini, usually only as far as Náxos (3¼ hrs. from Piraeus).

Except Sundays there are daily connections between Náxos and the Small Cyclades with the Skopelítis (next page).

Ship connections and bookings can be queried and undertaken in the Internet under *www.gtpnet.com*. Ship locations can be queried under *www.marinetraffic.com* or *www.shiptracking.eu*

㉞ Káto Koufonísi

"Káto", the "Lower" and slightly more tree-covered of the two Koufonísi Islands is not permanently inhabited, yet served by a small bathing boat every two hours in season. The boat, moreover, passes through a bizarre rocky bay on the north side of the island.
The 1½-hour walk leads from the boat's second landing stage back to the first one, where you wait for the return crossing in a tiny taverna. Deserted beaches and rock formations make the hike worthwhile.
■ ***3 km, difference in altitude 80m, easy***

AWT The long, grey-pebbled **Neró Bay** is the second place where the boat stops on the island. While most passengers are content to "lie" here, we head inland at the
0.00 tamarisk. Opposite the **cistern** begins an ascending path, which reaches the stony plateau after two minutes, where we at once turn off right. Up on the left are the ruins of a house – with solar panel. We proceed along goat tracks to
0.15 further **ruins** on a hillock 1 (**P1:** N36°54.396'/E25°35.546', 80m). There we enjoy a wonderful view back across Neró Bay and Schinoússa, Irakliá and Ios.
Between the ruins begins a clearly distinguishable track, which immediately runs past a round threshing area, an alóni (left). After a gap in the wall we drop down to Déti
0.25 Bay, accessible through juniper bushes and then a **gate** (**P2:** N36°54.746'/E25°34.826'). Again pebbles; so connoisseurs wait another five minutes and find, directly be-
0.30 hind the next climb, two small **sandy beaches.**
Up on top a holiday house later appears on the left, its owner letting the well-disposed hiker appreciate his wisdoms on boards. Passing the branch-off to Laki Bay, we ar-

1

2

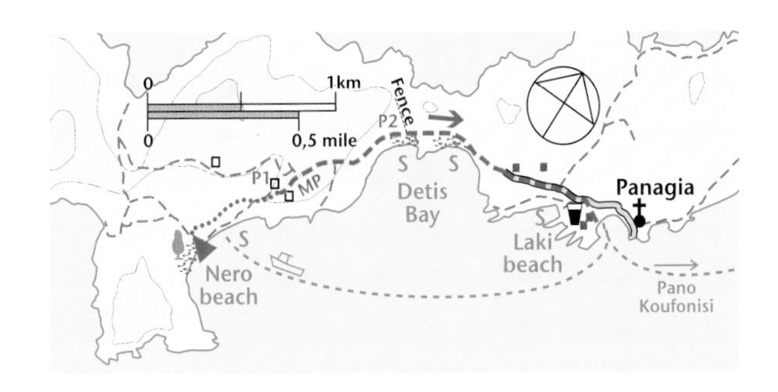

0.45 ★ rive at the **taverna** *Venezanos* ② – far and wide the most splendid place to wait for a ship! Elated we then skip down to the landing stage *Taverna.*

■ **Departures Skopelítis**

Tuesday – Thursday – Friday – (without ***Donoússa****)*
Katápola (Amorgós) 7.00, Koufonísi 8.30, Schinoússa 9.00, Iráklia 9.30, Náxos 11.00.

Monday – Wednesday – Saturday (via ***Donoússa****)*
Náxos 14.00, Iráklia 15.30, Schinoússa 16.00, Koufonísi 16.30, Donoússa 18.00, Katápola (Amorgós) 20.00.

Schinoússa

From the sea this member of the "Small Cyclades" looks more rugged than it actually is. It offers gently rolling hilly country, unusually wide fields and even pastures, little olive groves and vineyards - yet noticeably few chapels.
In recent years some mule tracks have been widened for the farmers' pickups and for holiday houses, though asphalt roads are still rare. In the evenings one has a good choice of stylishly furnished inns for fine dining.
Taxi: 0030 6973 215518

35 Three sandy coves

Almost entirely without inclines the 3½-hour hike crosses the bucolic north of the island and passes three remote coves. While the route has no springs, the taverna in Messariá may be open!
■ ***12 km, difference in altitude 135m, easy***

AWT 0.00 From the portal of the **Panagía church** (right) in **Chóra** you set off in a northerly direction, but at once turn off right at the corner and then left into the first alley. On the right you see the infirmary (Iatreio). Later islands and ilets float in the sea to the right. Walk straight ahead on the road, past a builder's shop (right), then over a hillock with the pension *Provalom* and down into farming land with isolated white houses.

0.12 Certainly you do not want to miss the **right branch-off** of a kalderími (**P1:** N36°50.365'/E25°28.135'). It leads di-

0.20 rectly to **Messariá**, a ghost village up until 2000 ①. In

front of the church you turn right, pass the taverna (left)
0.30 and follow the sign to the roadway leading to **Psilí-Ámmos Bay:** fine sand, tamarisks and glorious water!
Proceeding along easily identifiable tracks through the bushes, you walk on along the coastline at the dizzy height of about 30 to 50m above the jagged basalt rocks. After 8 min. you pass through a gap in the wall (**P2:** N36°52.860'/E25°31.849'). After that you move away from the sea and come to terraced fields. These can easily be traversed at the lower edge. Beyond the terraces it is possible to discern the highest mountain in the Cyclades, Mt. Zás or Zeus (1001 m), on Náxos. The next sandy
0.55 strand, secluded **Fikío Strand**, is not bad either!
On the left of the cattle-trough begins a dirt track heading towards a T-junction, where you turn left. (The monopáti to Messariá marked on the maps is overgrown.) Skirting the wide fields, you head along a dirt track in the direction of the windmill hill. You reach the main track through another gate. Follow this uphill 50m to the left, turning right on to a dirt track in front of a gate. Fairly soon this ends as a cul-de-sac in front of a gate, but to the right of that and to the right of a wall, you continue with-
1.20 out a path down to the sandy **cove of Gerolimiónas** 2.
★ With any luck you may have the 21m long beach to yourself.
The way back takes you up to the main track again and
1.40 then right, as far as a **cistern** (right). On the road you go left, turning right in front of the first house in Messariá on to the already familiar kalderími. **P1** takes you back to
2.00 **Chóra.**

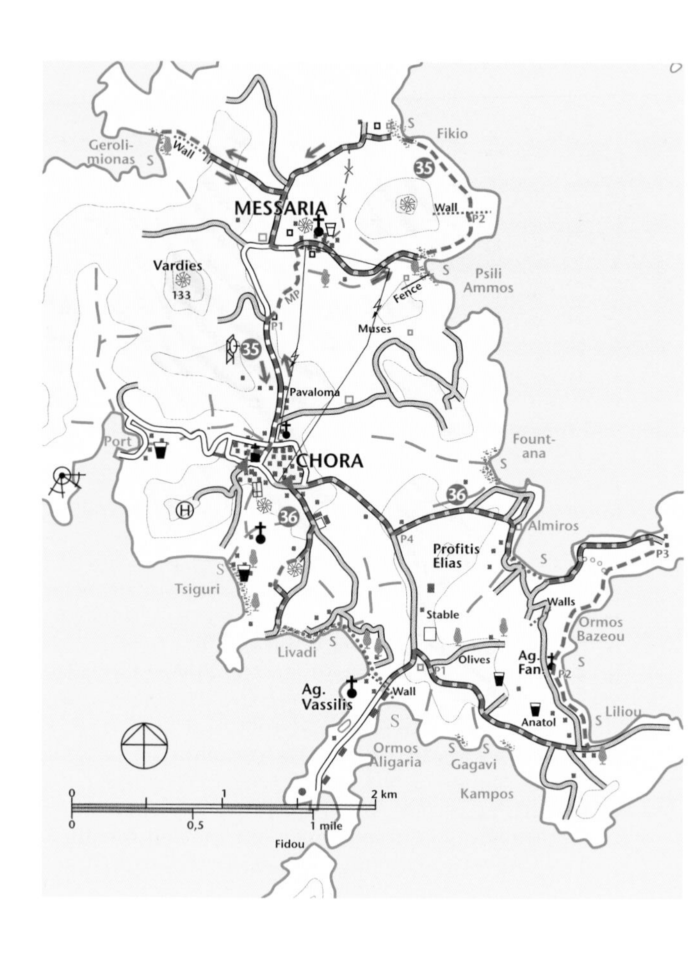

The rural island is renowned for its high-quality natural products, which are widely offered to guests. The most famous dish is *patatato,* a casserole with goat meat, potatoes and spices. Of course the island has its own recipes for fava, chickpea paste.

On the village alley as well as on Tsigoúri strand there are several sophisticated eateries which are well worth visiting. In addition at night the restaurant *Deli* offers a fantastic view over to twinkling Santoríni.

㊱ The secret …

… of the peninsula Agios Vassílios has never been completely uncovered. We will therefore pass by it at a respectful distance and later be devoting ourselves to easier tasks: a couple of beaches and the farming country of southern Schinóussa, 2½ hours, mostly following roadways, without any tavernas or wells.
■ 8 km, difference in altitude 75m, easy
▷ Map see left

AWT 0.00 Heading east out of **Chóra**, you come to a **fork** at the car park in front of the **hotel "Meltémi"** and descend right on to a roadway in the direction of Livadi. Ahead of us the Vassílios peninsula, which we will be concerned with afterwards [1]. After two minutes you turn right on to another roadway beside a beverage depot (left) and a *little later* !! *again!* Further down, 40m in front of a **windmill**, you 0.05 dart sideways to the right and a little further down find a roadway which turns off to the left. It joins a wide roadway dropping to the sea. Once at the water, you take a 0.20 well-beaten track left to **Livádi Beach.**

Opposite lies the Agios Vassílios peninsula. On the landward side you can see a wall with a tower. Further to the right is a gigantic water collection plant, at the top of which is another tower. Not exactly inviting …

"Treasure Island" was the title a big German daily paper gave to its story in 2006 about one of the largest scandals concerning art theft. The owner of the peninsula was a Greek-American art dealer who had since died under unexplained circumstances – a benefactor for the island, but whom nobody really knew. After a second unexplained death on Schinóussa and further suspicious circum-

1

2

stances, the police searched the peninsula. They found hundreds of ancient art objects of dubious origin, partly from Egypt. Leads were followed up to places as far away as a museum in Los Angeles. To this day not much is said about it on Schinóussa. In the meantime a nephew of the art dealer lives there.

At a safe distance you climb to the left of the wall, up a well-beaten track through a stonemasonary firm and

0.30 reach the **entrance gate**, which is nowadays open. But you are warned to mind the dog in many languages!

So it is best to climb up to the main track and right there in the direction of Lióliou. The branch-off at a cistern (**P1:** N36°52.860'/E25°31.848') leaves us untouched despite the inviting landscape, likewise the next one. In a dip

0.50 with holiday houses the roadway ends at the sandy **beach of Lióliou** ②. Tamarisks remind us it is time for a rest.

Mostly on flat rock we then continue along Bazéos bay.

1.00 The tiny altar church of **St. Fanourious** (**P2:** N36°51.700'/E25°32.173') stands beside the secure path. Inland is a taverna. After a fence you could try your luck by going left over a hill by way of a shortcut. If you stay by the water,

1.15 you come to **holiday houses** made of grey quarry stone (**P3:** N36°52.005'/E25°32.500'). From here you use the

1.25 coastal roadway to the bathing beach on **Almyrós Bay.** Visible out at sea is the uninhabited Káto Koufonísi and beyond it the popular bathing island of Epáno Koufonísi. From the cistern on the bay you climb up to the main trail (**P4:** N36°52.016'/E25°31.582') and then on right up to

1.50 **Chóra**, also known as **Panagía.**

Overview Übersicht Coup d'œil

Naxos

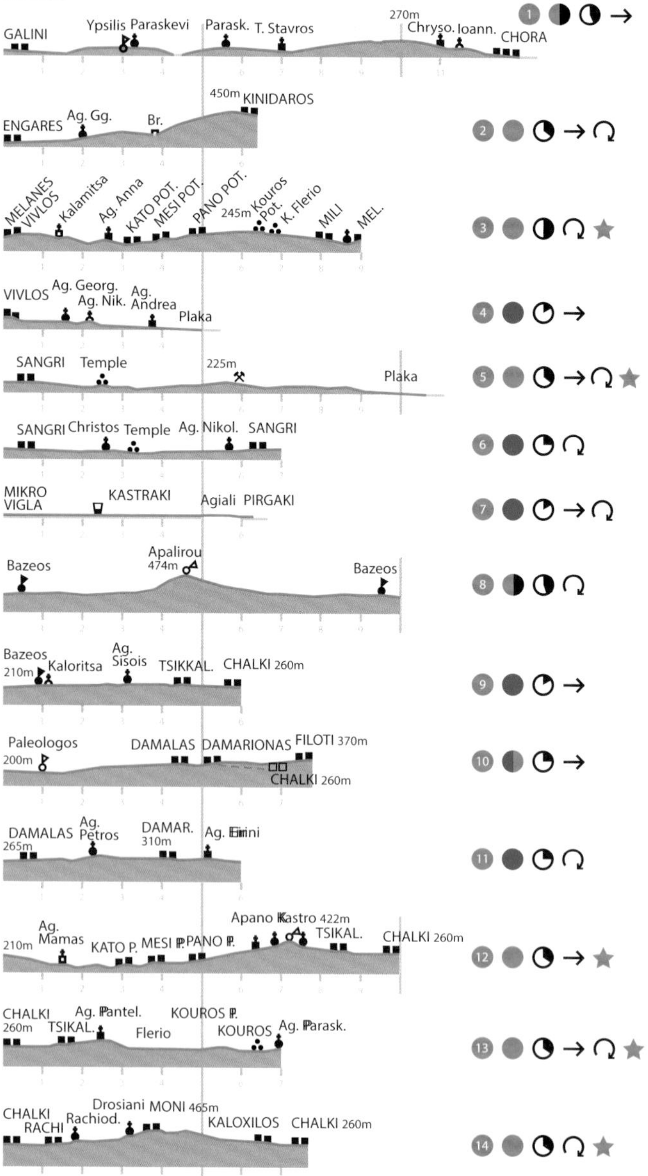

1
GALINI Ypsilis Paraskevi Parask. T. Stavros 270m Chryso. Ioann. CHORA

2
ENGARES Ag. Gg. Br. 450m KINIDAROS

3
MELANES VIVLOS Kalamitsa Ag. Anna KATO POT. MESI POT. PANO POT. 245m Kouros Pot. K. Flerio MILI MEL.

4
VIVLOS Ag. Georg. Ag. Nik. Ag. Andrea Plaka

5
SANGRI Temple 225m Plaka

6
SANGRI Christos Temple Ag. Nikol. SANGRI

7
MIKRO VIGLA KASTRAKI Agiali PIRGAKI

8
Bazeos Apalirou 474m Bazeos

9
Bazeos 210m Kaloritsa Ag. Sisois TSIKKAL. CHALKI 260m

10
Paleologos 200m DAMALAS DAMARIONAS FILOTI 370m CHALKI 260m

11
DAMALAS 265m Ag. Petros DAMAR. 310m Ag. Eirini

12
210m Ag. Mamas KATO P. MESI P. PANO P. Apano Kastro 422m TSIKAL. CHALKI 260m

13
CHALKI 260m TSIKAL. Ag. Pantel. Flerio KOUROS P. KOUROS Ag. Parask.

14
CHALKI RACHI Rachiod. Drosiani MONI 465m KALOXILOS CHALKI 260m

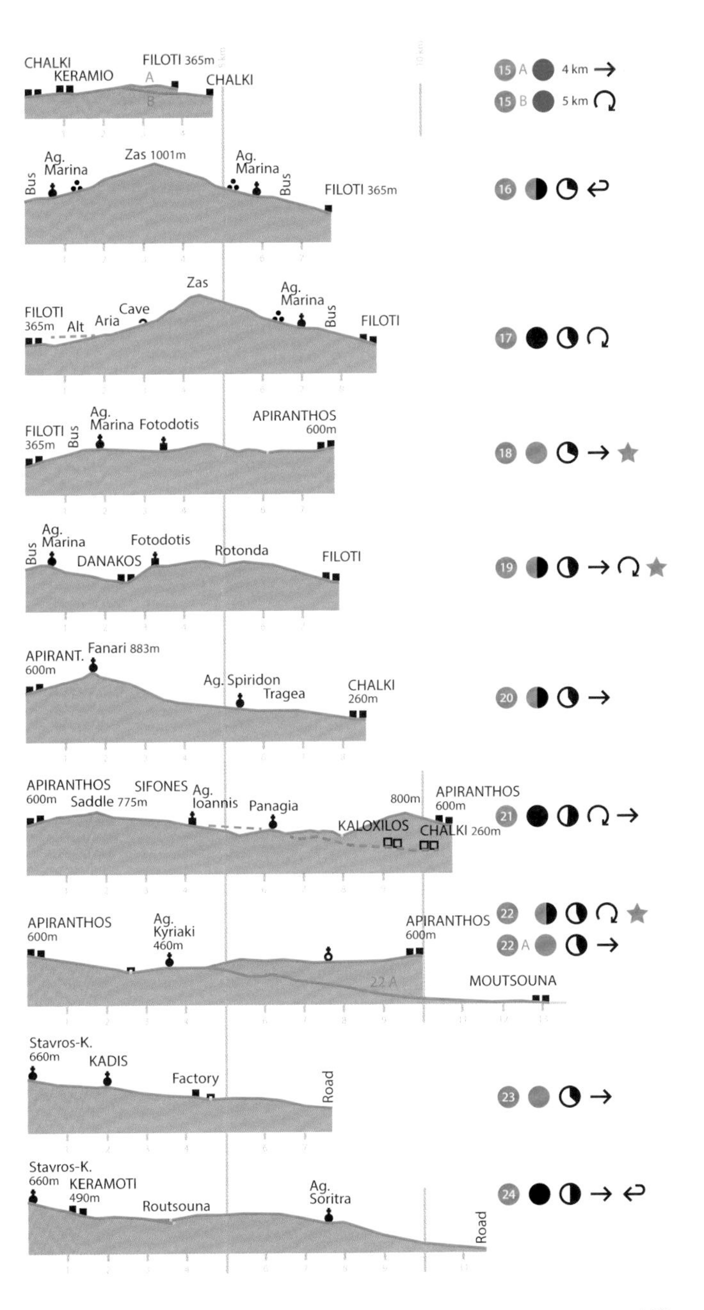
CHALKI
KERAMIO
FILOTI 365m
A
B
CHALKI
15 A 4 km
15 B 5 km
Ag. Marina
Bus
Zas 1001m
Ag. Marina
Bus
FILOTI 365m
16
FILOTI 365m
Alt
Aria
Cave
Zas
Ag. Marina
Bus
FILOTI
17
FILOTI 365m
Bus
Ag. Marina
Fotodotis
APIRANTHOS 600m
18
Bus
Ag. Marina
DANAKOS
Fotodotis
Rotonda
FILOTI
19
APIRANT. 600m
Fanari 883m
Ag. Spiridon
Tragea
CHALKI 260m
20
APIRANTHOS 600m
Saddle 775m
SIFONES
Ag. Ioannis
Panagia
800m
KALOXILOS
APIRANTHOS 600m
CHALKI 260m
21
APIRANTHOS 600m
Ag. Kyriaki 460m
22 A
APIRANTHOS 600m
MOUTSOUNA
22
22 A
Stavros-K. 660m
KADIS
Factory
Road
23
Stavros-K. 660m
KERAMOTI 490m
Routsouna
Ag. Soritra
Road
24

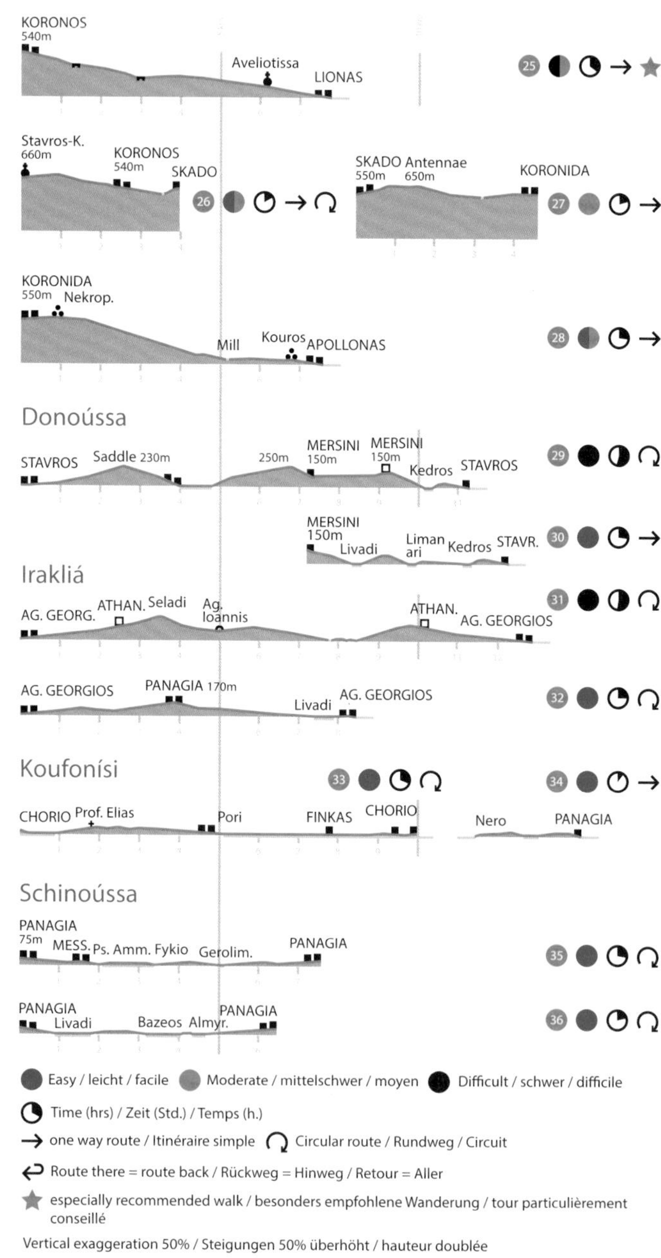
KORONOS
540m
Aveliotissa
LIONAS
25
Stavros-K.
660m
KORONOS
540m
SKADO
26
SKADO Antennae
550m 650m
KORONIDA
27
KORONIDA
550m Nekrop.
Mill
Kouros
APOLLONAS
28
Donoússa
STAVROS
Saddle 230m
250m
MERSINI
150m
MERSINI
150m
Kedros
STAVROS
29
MERSINI
150m
Livadi
Liman
ari
Kedros
STAVR.
30
Irakliá
AG. GEORG.
ATHAN.
Seladi
Ag.
Ioannis
ATHAN.
AG. GEORGIOS
31
AG. GEORGIOS
PANAGIA 170m
Livadi
AG. GEORGIOS
32
Koufonísi
33
34
CHORIO
Prof. Elias
Pori
FINKAS
CHORIO
Nero
PANAGIA
Schinoússa
PANAGIA
75m
MESS.
Ps. Amm.
Fykio
Gerolim.
PANAGIA
35
PANAGIA
Livadi
Bazeos
Almyr.
PANAGIA
36
Easy / leicht / facile
Moderate / mittelschwer / moyen
Difficult / schwer / difficile
Time (hrs) / Zeit (Std.) / Temps (h.)
one way route / Itinéraire simple
Circular route / Rundweg / Circuit
Route there = route back / Rückweg = Hinweg / Retour = Aller
especially recommended walk / besonders empfohlene Wanderung / tour particulièrement conseillé
Vertical exaggeration 50% / Steigungen 50% überhöht / hauteur doublée

Abbreviations, Key

	hiking route on a road or dirt track
	hiking route on a street
	hiking route on a path
	hiking route without a path
ALT	alternative route, short-cut
← ←	walking direction / alternative
P	GPS-point
	street
	dirt road, sandy track
MP 4	monopáti, kalderími, mule track, marking
	dry streambed (at times), hollow
	antenna
	bus stop / seasonal
P	parking area / parking your hire car
H S	helicopter landing pad / solar plant
	cemetery
+	wayside shrine, monument
	sports field
	cave
	medieval castle, dwelling tower / ruins
	ancient ruins, statue
	houses / ruins
	monastery, large church / ruins
	chapel / summit chapel / ruins
	taverna / open seasonally
	windmill, ruins / watermill
	fountain, well, spring, reservoir, cistern
S	swimming possible
In the text: ①	Reference to another hike
	Steep passage, possible feelings of vertigo
OW	time for walking one way
!!	pay attention to turn-off!
★	the author's 18 favourite spots

Some Greek words for hikers:

Stress on the accents.

jássas	**hello**
ne	yes
óchi	no
parakaló	please
efcharistó	thank you
endáxi	okay
sto kaló	all the best
kalá	lovely
símera	today
ávrio	tomorrow
pósin óra?	How long?
pósso makriá ine ja?	How far is it to...?
puíne...?	Where is...?
óra	hour
neró	water
psomí	bread
tirí	cheese
míkro	small
mégalo	big
leoforió	bus
stásis	bus stop
enikáso	rent
aftókinito	auto
mechanáki	motor bike
podílato	bicycle
kaíki	boat
chora	**city**
chorio	hamlet
spíti	house
platía	square
parélia	harbour promenade
kástro	Venetian castle
pírgos	fortified Venetian castle
nekrotafío	cemetery
limáni	harbour
vrísi	fountain
stérna	cistern
kafenío	café, and how!
eklisiá	**church**
papás	priest
moní, monastíri	monastery
ksoklísi	chapel
panagía	Mother of God
panigíri	parish fair
ágios, agía, AG	saint
ikonostasio	icon altar screen
katholikón	central building in a monastery

kerós	weather
aéras	wind
meltémi	strong north wind
ílios	sun
wrochí	rain
omíchli	fog
níssos	island
farángi, langádi	ravine, gorge
kámpos, pláka	plains
livádi	meadow
déndro	tree
léfkes	poplars
dássos	forest
lófos	hill
wounó, óros	mountain
vígla	mountain peak
vráches	rock, cliff
spíleo	cave
thálassa	sea
órmos	bay
límni	lake
potámi	river
réma	dry bed
pigí	spring
pérazma	pass, ridge
xirolithía	dry wall
odiporió	**wandering**
isía	straight on
dexiá	right
aristerá	left
apáno	uphill
káto	downhill
kondá	near
makriá	far
ásfalto	asphalt street
drómos	street
chomaódromos	gravel street
dasikí odós	forest path
odós	path
skála	path of steps
monopáti	mule track
kalderími	paved way
katsikó drómos	goat path
yéfira	bridge
stavrodrómi	crossing, intersection
hártis	map
kutrúmbulo	path marking
phrygana	scrub, the island hiker's enemy

Index of places   Ortsindex   Index des noms de lieu

Náxos